Hats Made Easy

MILNER CRAFT SERIES

Hats Made Easy

LYN WARING

SALLY MILNER PUBLISHING

First published in 1995 by
Sally Milner Publishing Pty Ltd
558 Darling Street
Rozelle NSW 2039 Australia

© Lyn Waring 1995

Illustrations by Stephanie Cooper
Photography by Andrew Elton
Make up by Julie Elton
Styling by Louise Owens
Cover colour separation by Sphere Color Graphics
Inside colour pages separation by Dah Hua Printing, Hong Kong
Printed in Australia by Impact Printing

National Library of Australia
Cataloguing-in-Publication data:

Waring, Lyn.
    Hats made easy

    ISBN 1 86351 150 4

    1. Hats. 2. Millinery. I. Title.

646.504

Hat blocks from The Mosman Antique Centre
700 Military Road, Mosman NSW 2088 (02) 968 1319

Covered hat box and teddy bears from Lois With Love
165 Middle Head Road Mosman NSW 2088 (02) 969 6847

DEDICATION

To George, with love and appreciation

ACKNOWLEDGEMENTS

My sincere thanks to Stephanie Cooper for her patience and understanding in transforming and making my sketches, photos and samples into respectable diagrams.

My thanks to Kay Platts, Lecturer in Fashion at the Bentley College of TAFE, for reading through the draft and for her helpful suggestions.

My apologies to Puss, my dog and faithful companion, who thought I was cross with her when I was abusing the computer while trying to match the graphics with the text.

Thank you David Pannell for explaining, simply, how to combine graphics and text.

My thanks to the makers of the special fabrics, Deborah Combes for the machine knits; Nancy Ballesteros for the silk felt; Judith Pinnell for the machine embroidery; Judith Shaw for the handmade felt.

A special thank you to all the staff at Sally Milner Publishing. They encouraged and guided me through a task I thought was going to be easy.

And lastly, a very special thank you to our models, Blair Duarte, Caroline and Rebecca.

Polyurethane 'collars' are now available and for enquiries about distributors, please telephone (02) 949 7477, or fax (02) 948 5987.

CONTENTS

COLOUR PLATE CAPTIONS

PLATE 1   Below left: Beret 2, machine embroidered
Centre: Beret 2, in leather
Above left: Beret 2, wool/silk handmade felt, machine embellished
Above right: Beret 2, handmade felt, machine stitched
Below right: Beret 2, handmade felt
Inset: Beret 2, machine-knit fabric

PLATE 2   Below left and right: Basic brim, slightly narrowed at top and basic brim widened
Centre: Basic crown
Above left and right: Basic crown extended and scrunched down
Inset: Basic crown shortened, basic brim widened

PLATE 3   Main picture and inset: Basic beret with bandeau and peak

PLATE 4   Inset, below left and above right: Basic crown heightened and then widened at the top.
Basic brim widened
Below right: Basic crown heightened and widened, machine stitched

PLATE 5   Above left: 3-piece round crown with peak, in cotton
Below left: 3-piece round crown with brim and pleat in centre crown
Below right: 3-piece round crown with brim and pleat in centre crown
Inset: 3-piece round crown with peak, in handmade felt

PLATE 6   Inset and top right: Basic crown heightened and widened at top, with brim modified
to sit closer to face, then shortened
Centre: Basic crown widened
Below left and above left (partially hidden): Basic crown widened with basic under beret for brim
Below right: Basic crown heightened, then scrunched down with shortened brim.

PLATE 7   Above left: 5-piece crown. Basic under beret for brim, with brim down
Below left: 5-piece crown. Basic under beret for brim, with brim up
Above right: 5-piece crown with basic brim modified to sit close to face or turned up
Below right: 3-piece crown with peak
Inset: 6-piece crown

PLATE 8   Below left: 6-piece beret in machine-knit fabric
Below right: 6-piece beret in silk felt paper
Below centre: 6-piece beret
Top left: 6-piece beret, knit fabric
Top right: 6-piece beret with peak
Inset: 6-piece beret

PLATE 9   Inset and below left: Basic crown, narrowed slightly at top, with basic brim modified to be flatter
Centre: As above, tartan, in man's size
Below right: Basic crown, narrowed at top, with basic under beret as brim
Top left: Basic crown, narrowed slightly at top, heightened with basic brim shortened slightly

PLATE 10   Main picture and inset: Basic crown with brim extended to the limit of practicality

PLATE 11   Below right: Basic crown with basic brim, machine embroidered
Below left: Basic crown, with basic brim in handmade felt
Above, left and right: Basic crown
Centre: Basic crown, extended and scrunched down
Inset: Basic crown, with basic brim and organdy bow trim

PLATE 12   Create your own design.

INTRODUCTION

Hats are a very important part of our everyday wardrobe. They are inexpensive to make and, with a little experience, individual designs can be created in a relatively short time. I have always enjoyed making hats and creating my own designs and I am eager to share my joy of hat-making with others.

By using the patterns in this book and following the step-by-step instructions, you will be able to make a hat that is individual, your own creation and your size! No matter how often you use the same pattern, you'll find that you can make it look different every time – by changing the fabric or adding some trim. By following the instructions on how to modify a basic pattern, you can alter the shape and have your own completely original design.

The methods of hat-making I have described are from my own experience of making fabric hats with the basic equipment. Materials and equipment, of course, will vary with each design.

They can also be made unique by using one of the many textile craft techniques – paint or print on fabric, simple block prints, machine knit fabric, machine embroidery, hand embroidery, patchwork, appliqué, handmade felt and combinations of these.

MEASUREMENTS

The measurements in this book are in metric with the closest conversion to inches in brackets ("). There can be slight variances in the transition, however, you the designer can make an educated decision when calculating for your own specific designs.

The first concern when making a hat is the size of the head.

1

The first head measurement, and the one generally referred to, should be taken around the head. With a tape measure, from the mid-centre forehead, go around behind the ear, over the bump at the back and continue on behind the other ear, back to the mid-centre forehead where you started. This measurement determines the size of the hat needed to fit the head.(diagrams 1 & 2)

2

Next we need to know the depth of the head. There are two head-depth measurements which enable you to determine the depth of the crown of your hat design:

3

• ear to ear – taken from behind the front ear, over the top of the head to behind the ear on the other side. (diagram 3)

• front to back – from the mid-centre forehead, toward the back, over the top of the head to the bump at the back of the head. (diagram 4)

The head is an oval shape, though it may look round. For the projects in this book, the head measurement is 56 cm (22") ear-to-ear measurement is 34 cm (13⅜") front to back measurement is 36 cm (14¼").

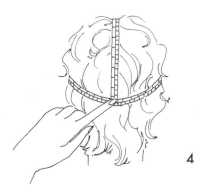

4

EQUIPMENT

The first basic piece of equipment required is a 'collar'. The collar is an oval piece of wood about 2 cm (¾") in thickness, with a hole in the middle. The circumference is the head measurement (in this case, 56 cm or 22"). (diagram 5) A dome-shape millinery block can also be used.

Outlines of the various sizes of collar are included in the back of this book. Use one of these as a template to cut out the size you need for your hat-making projects. It is best if it is cut from a soft wood, like pine, because you will be pushing drawing pins into it quite often. You could use compressed hardboard, but the edge may catch a little and after a time, there may not be sufficient 'wood' to grip the drawing pins.

If you have difficulty finding a collar, you can cut out several cardboard collars. Cut the centre hole as well, then glue them together and wrap a wide adhesive tape around the edge. It is also inexpensive and easy to replace.

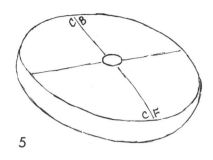

5

You also need a 'stand', a heavy base on which you place the collar when making a hat. Mine is a solid piece of wood 10 cm (4") square and 8 cm (3⅛") high. It has a metal rod about pencil thickness protruding 5 cm (2") from the centre. The hole in the collar sits over the metal rod. (diagram 6)

To make an improvised stand, fill an empty food tin about 10 cm (4") in diameter with wet cement or plaster. Before it sets, stick a piece of metal rod, a pencil or something similar, into the centre so it protrudes about 5 cm (2") above the edge of the tin. You can also fill a lidded food tin with sand and hammer a rod, or something similar, into the centre of the lid. Be sure to tape the lid on with strong adhesive tape because it isn't much fun if you drop the tin.

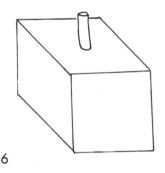

6

FABRICS

Lightweight fabrics, such as cotton, cotton blends, lightweight linen, fine wool, wool blends and rayon, were used for the projects in this book. These types of fabrics are the easiest to use when you're learning to make hats but, as you gain experience, try different ones. You can buy remnants quite cheaply and they are usually big enough to make a small hat. You'll find some synthetics can be difficult to work with and will require more patience.

If you decide on a thicker or heavier fabric, like velvet, canvas or corded velvet, add 2 to 2.5 cm (¾" to 1") to the head measurement. Thicker fabrics create more bulk around the collar edge when attaching the brim to the crown and the hat will be too small for the head.

Hats also look great in hand-crafted fabrics and textiles – hand and machine embroidery, patchwork, quilting, handmade felt, woven fabrics, hand and machine knitting, silk-screened designs, appliqué, hand-painted fabrics, handmade paper, and whatever else comes to mind.

INTERFACING

Vilene is a non-woven interfacing which is used to stabilise the pattern pieces and to stiffen where necessary. There are two types – fusible and non-fusible – and they come in a variety of weights or thicknesses. Various weights of Vilene are good to have on hand although I find medium weight is the most useful.

Fusible has a coating on one side and will adhere to fabric when a hot iron is applied to it. Use either a steam iron or a dry iron, at cotton temperature – I use a pressing cloth. It is very important to test first, using a reasonable-sized piece of fabric and Vilene.

Non-fusible does not have a coating and is preferred with some fabrics, particularly synthetics which do not like a hot iron. It is sometimes necessary to tack the non-fusible Vilene to the fabric pattern piece.

WADDING

Wadding is fabric that gives your hat form and body. It is commonly used for quilting and comes in a variety of thicknesses and widths. The type I have used in this book is referred to as 'apparel wadding' and is 0.5 cm (¼") thick and 70 cm (28") wide with a firm surface on both sides. Fusible wadding is also available in a variety of thicknesses.

If you only have the thicker type, peel it apart to the thickness required. The inner side will be a bit fluffy so place the firmer side to the fabric.

TRIMS

I haven't covered possible trims in this book – there are so many good books and magazines that deal with the multitude of techniques for trimming hats.

I just love the silk flowers that are available these days, particularly the type that are used in vases. You can modify these quite easily to suit a hat – and don't throw away the leaves which can look great with just some ribbons.

Give your hats that special touch that is just 'you' and make your designs individual. Hats are fun, very practical and they make wonderful gifts, so enjoy making them. I do!

BASIC EQUIPMENT AND MATERIALS

- Collar

- Stand

- Tape measure

- Lightweight paper – years ago I used old newspapers

- Tracing paper

- Medium-grade paper, if you are going to grade the size of your hat

- Lightweight card to transfer your often-used pattern, and to grade sizes

- Tracing wheel

- Drawing pins

- Coloured pencils

- Felt pens – a few colours are useful

- Lead pencil

- Rulers – 1 straight, 1 set square

- Sticky tape – the type you can write on is best

- Glue – stick glue is the easiest to use

- Scissors – 1 pair for paper and 1 pair for fabric

- Dressmakers' pins, needles and thread to match the fabric

- Dressmakers' fading felt tip marking pen is useful (optional)

- Sewing machine

- Fabric for making the toile

- Fabric for making the final hat

- Vilene – non-woven interfacing

- Wadding

- Trims – ribbons, flowers and all sorts of bits and pieces to make your design very special

CHAPTER 1

THE BASIC BRIM

In this chapter we will go step-by-step through the process of making a basic brim. After completing this project you will be able to create your own brim designs.

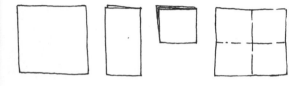

1

The head measurement for this exercise is 56 cm (22").

Fold a 45 cm (17¾") square of paper into quarters. Draw a line on the length of each fold line. (diagram 1)

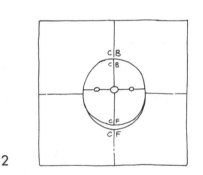

2

Place the collar on the paper, aligning the marks on the collar with the lines on the paper. Draw a line around the collar, then remove the collar. (diagram 2)

Inside the collar line, measure in 1.5 cm (⅝") seam allowance. On the centre line mark C/F (centre front) and C/B (centre back). (diagram 3)

Now decide the depth of the brim.

The general rule is that the back brim is shorter than the front. If they were the same the brim would look lop-sided. I like to make the sides halfway between the C/F and C/B measurements.

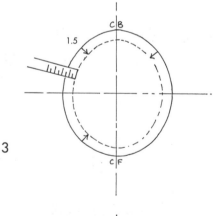

3

The measurements are out from collar line:
- front   10 cm (4")
- back   8 cm (3⅛")
- sides   9 cm (3½")
- side/front   9.5 cm (3¾")
- side/back   8.5 cm (3⅜")

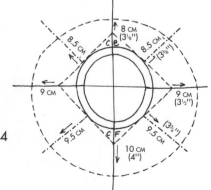

4

Measure and mark halfway between the sides and front, and sides and back, by placing a ruler just touching the collar edge. Square a line straight out from this point toward the brim edge. You now have the brim outline. (diagram 4)

The following diagrams are specifically to do with the collar edge so the brim outline has been omitted for the sake of space.

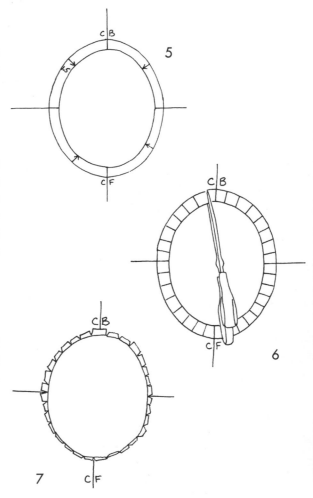

Cut out the inner section of the collar, leaving the seam allowance (diagram 5). Clip into the collar seam allowance to the collar line every 1 to 1.25 cm (³⁄₈"). Clip either side the C/F, C/B and side lines, as these points are important in aligning the brim to the crown when sewing the hat together. Clip all the way around the collar seam allowance. (diagram 6)

Lift each clipped section and fold back onto the collar line. Flatten them back and then lift them upright. Leave this brim draft on a flat surface while you continue. (diagram 7)

THE HEADBAND/BANDEAU

Cut a strip of paper which is the length of the head measurement + 2 cm (³⁄₄") for overlap x 3 cm (1¹⁄₈").

Fold the strip of paper in half lengthways, then in half crossways. The crease line becomes the C/F.

Our example is:
58 cm long x 3 cm wide (22⁷⁄₈" long x 1¹⁄₈" wide). (diagram 8)

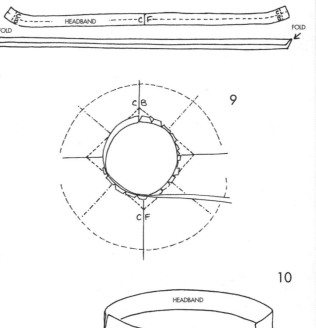

Unfold the headband, place one edge to the inside of the clipped edge on the collar seam allowance on the brim draft. Pin at the C/F crease, in line with the C/F of the collar edge seam allowance and ease the headband around the edge to the C/B, overlapping the end of the headband 1 cm (³⁄₈"), and secure with a pin at the C/B. Fold the headband over the upright clipped collar edge. (diagrams 9 & 10)

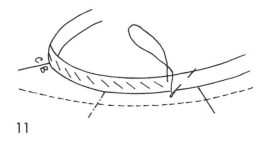

11

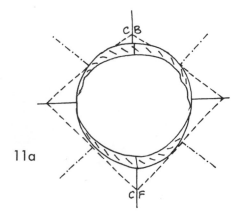

11a

With a needle and double thread, stitch the headband to the collar edge with a stab stitch, in and out, on an angle, to hold the two together. (diagrams 11 & 11a)

As you gain more experience you will be able to stick the headband to the collar seam allowance with glue. Staples can also be a quick method.

If this is your first time making a hat, please sew it to the collar seam allowance.

12

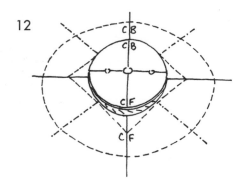

Place the collar in the headband of the brim, C/F and C/B aligned. Secure with drawing pins at C/F, C/B and sides, and place on stand. (diagram 12)

Now begin to shape the brim.

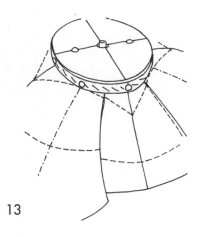

13

Cut into the paper, between C/F and side line, from brim into the collar edge, overlapping these by 0.5 cm (¼") approximately, and securing with sticky tape at brim and collar edge.

Repeat this on the other side, then move to between C/B and side. Repeat the process around the brim until it is the shape you want. (diagram 13)

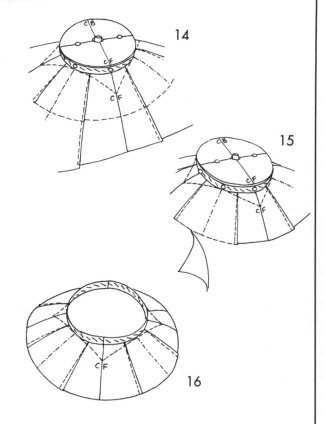

14

15

It is a good idea to take little and often when shaping the brim. The more overlaps you make in the brim the closer to the face it will sit. This means it will be more 'drooped' and can be turned back or up. Remember to stand back and look at the shape as you go.

If you want to change the depth, draw a new brim edge outline to the required depth. When your brim depth is to your liking, cut off the excess paper on the design line. (diagrams 14 & 15)

Remove brim and collar from stand, take out the drawing pins and carefully lift collar out of the brim. (diagram 16)

16

Cut up C/B line from brim edge to collar line. Carefully cut around collar line to remove the headband. (diagrams 17 & 18)

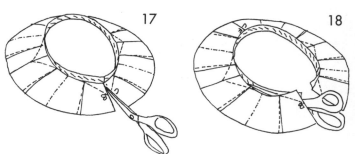

17

18

You now have a brim pattern without seam allowances. (diagram 19)

Redraw the brim outline to smooth out any bumps or dips that can be a result of the overlapping, and likewise around the collar edge.

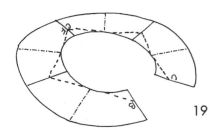

19

TRANSFER TO PATTERN

Fold a piece of pattern paper in half. Place brim pattern piece over pattern paper, with C/F fold line in line with folded edge of pattern paper. Some people work best from the left, others the right – whichever is comfortable for you. However, because our design is symmetrical you only need to transfer one side of the brim. (diagram 20)

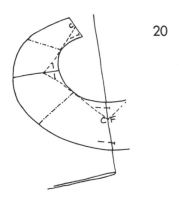

20

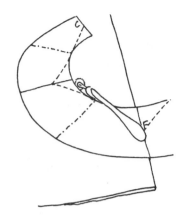

21

Pin the brim to the pattern paper and transfer, or trace, the brim outline to the paper.

Remove brim from pattern paper.

Add seam allowances:
- 1 cm (³⁄₈") to C/B
- 1.5 cm (⁵⁄₈") to collar edge
- 0.5 cm (¼") to brim edge.

Unfold your pattern paper and check the folded line at C/F. This can sometimes have a dip down, or a bump up. Now is the time to smooth this into a rounded line, at the brim edge and at the collar edge. (diagram 21)

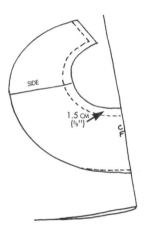

22

To avoid dip up and dip down, 'square' edge in from the C/F edge by 0.75 cm (¼" to ³⁄₈") at both the brim and collar edge.

Fold on C/F line again, and transfer or trace any alterations. (diagram 22)

Remember to mark C/F, C/B and side notches
at collar edge and brim edge.

When you are satisfied with the shape, cut out your pattern. (diagram 23)

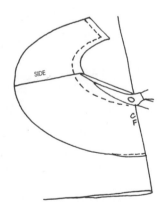

23

The straight grain

This indicates the correct placement of the pattern, in line with the straight weave of the fabric.

The straight grain of the brim can be parallel to the C/F line or on a bias to the C/F. It is up to you to decide which position is the most suited to your brim design and the fabric pattern. If the brim is to be worn rolled up or pushed back, have the bias at the position where the brim is to be rolled up or pushed back.

For a bias at the C/F, place a set square on the C/F line.

Mark an equal distance on each edge of the set square and draw a line connecting these marks. (diagram 24)

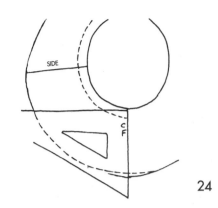

24

It is useful to note both of these positions on your pattern. Write 'straight grain' along the line. The bias is now at the front of the brim. (diagram 25)

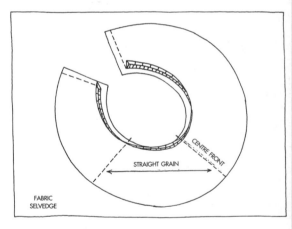

25

THE HEADBAND

We need to make a headband/bandeau to hold the brim in shape while trying on for design, and also for comfort. Measure the length of the collar stitch line on the collar edge of the brim. (diagram 26)

Decide the depth of the bandeau. If the finished depth is 3 cm (1⅛") it needs to be doubled because the headband/bandeau is folded.

Then add the collar edge seam allowance and double it:

3 x 2 = 6 + 3 cm S/A = 9 cm
(1⅛" x 2¼" = 6 + 1⅛" S/A = 3½").

Our example finishes as:
56 cm + 2 cm = 58 cm length x 9 cm width
(22" + ¾" = 22¾" length x 3⅜" width). (diagram 27)

26

Onto pattern paper, measure and mark 9 cm (3⅜") x 58 cm (22¾").

Divide the length in half – 29 cm (11⅜") – this becomes the C/F. Measure the distance between C/F and C/B and mark the side measurement to correspond with collar edge measurement.

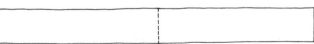

27

Now you can try out your first pattern by making a fabric toile.

MAKING A TOILE

MATERIALS AND EQUIPMENT

- Fashion fabric
- Vilene – fusible/iron-on, medium-weight non-woven interfacing
- Scissors
- Pins
- Sewing thread to match
- Sewing machine
- Iron
- Pressing cloth

28

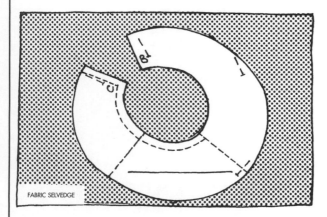

FABRIC SELVEDGE

Cut one brim pattern in fabric and one in medium-weight Vilene. (diagram 28) Because of the bias, the fabric can go out of shape. The pattern piece becomes more stable when it is fused to Vilene.

Bond the fabric and Vilene together.

Lay the Vilene down on an ironing surface, adhesive side up. Then lay the fabric down over the Vilene, right side up. Ease the fabric to fit the Vilene. Lay the pressing cloth over the brim and **press**.

29

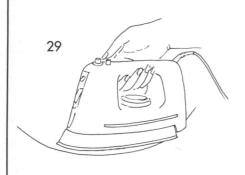

To press, you place the iron down and then lift it up off the fabric. Do not go back and forth as you would normally, as you could stretch the fabric pattern piece out of shape. (diagrams 29 & 29a)

29a

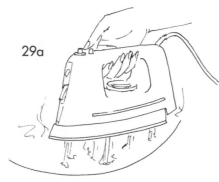

Alternatively, you can bond the fabric and Vilene together in one whole piece of fabric and then cut out your brim pattern. (If you are using non-fusible Vilene, carefully fit the fabric to the Vilene, then pin in place. Stitch the fabric to the Vilene.)

You now have one brim section. Sew the C/B seam with 1 cm (⅜") seam allowance. Press seam open. (diagram 30)

30

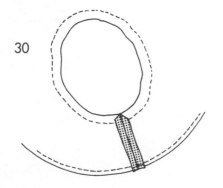

Cut one headband/bandeau in fabric. Sew the C/B seam and press seam open. Pin headband/bandeau to collar edge seam, joining at C/B seam, and C/F and sides. Ease and pin to fit.

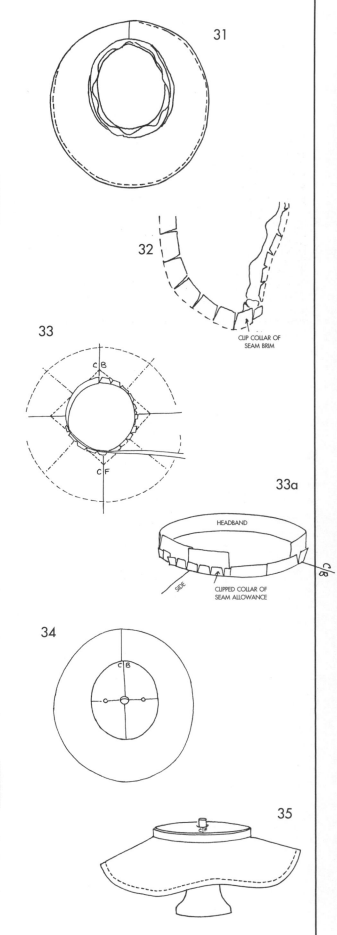

Remember the bandeau is on the straight of the fabric and the collar edge has a bias. They will fit if your measurements are correct, so go slowly and patiently.

Sew together with a long machine stitch – it is easier to unpick if alterations are necessary. (diagram 31)

Remember a 1.5 cm (⅝") seam allowance.

Clip into the collar/brim edge seam allowance, to within approximately 2 to 3 mm (¹⁄₁₆") of stitching line. (diagram 32)

Do not cut the bandeau.

Fold the bandeau over and stitch down to encase the clipped collar edge. (diagrams 33 & 33a)

Place collar into the bandeau of the fabric brim, aligning C/B and C/F, etc. (diagram 34)

Place collar and brim on the stand. Stand back and have a critical look at your brim, and at the shape. (diagram 35)

Make any modifications that may be necessary and mark these on the brim with a felt pen. If the brim is a bit floppy, pin out the fullness with little tucks at the appropriate places. If it is a bit too close to the head, mark where the adjustment is to be made.

Remove brim from stand and then remove the collar from the bandeau. Transfer any changes on the brim to the paper pattern.

Redraw brim outline if necessary and if the paper pattern is untidy, recut it.

Remember to mark C/F, C/B and sides.

You now have a basic brim pattern. Write your design details on the paper pattern for easy identification, e.g. small sketch of brim design, size, cut 2 fabric, cut 2 Vilene, cut 1 wadding, and remember straight grain lines. (We will need the wadding for the complete brim design.)

CHAPTER 2

THE BASIC CROWN

In this chapter, we go step-by-step through making a one piece side crown and top crown which will fit the basic brim.

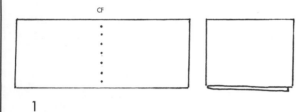

1

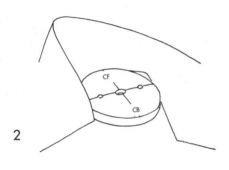

2

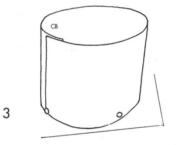

3

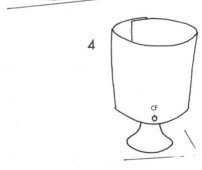

4

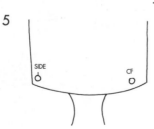

5

The head measurement for this exercise is 56 cm (22").

THE SIDE CROWN

Cut a piece of paper a little wider than the desired height of crown by the length of the head measurement plus 5 cm (2"). Fold paper in half widthways and crease. The crease line becomes C/F. (diagram 1)

Place the strip of paper around the collar in line with the collar edge. (diagram 2)

Secure with drawing pins, at the C/F crease first. Put a drawing pin at each side, then overlap the paper at C/B. (diagram 3)

Place collar and paper crown on stand. (diagram 4)

Looking inside the paper crown to the collar, mark with a felt pen on the paper crown collar edge the C/F, sides and C/B to correspond with these points on the collar. A felt pen marks best. The marks are on the outside of the paper crown in the accompanying diagram. (diagram 5)

Remove crown from collar and lay the paper crown flat. (diagram 6)

6

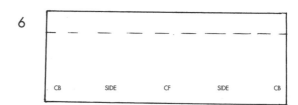

From the edge where the C/F, C/B and side marks are, measure the collar depth (the thickness of the wooden collar) from the bottom edge, and rule a line along this edge. This becomes the collar edge. From the collar edge, square a line up on paper crown, at the marks for C/B, C/F and sides. (diagram 7)

7

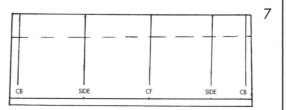

Measure halfway between these lines and draw a line straight through from bottom edge to top edge of paper crown. These are the 'cut' lines and are where we cut into the paper to create our side crown shape. (diagram 8)

8

Along these lines, cut from the top of the side crown to within 1 mm ($^1/_{16}$") of the collar edge, then from the bottom edge to within 1 mm ($^1/_{16}$") of the collar edge. On your first attempt, cut one line at a time.

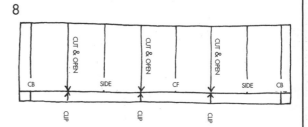

Make sure you do not cut right through.

Lay this over a new piece of paper – it will make the next step a little easier.

9

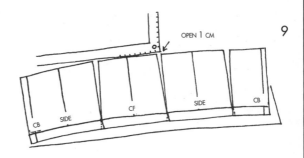

Carefully, at the top edge of the paper crown, open a cut out by 1 cm ($^3/_8$") and stick down both sides to the paper underneath to hold in place. The sticky tape you can write on is best. You will notice the cut at the bottom edge has folded over itself slightly. Secure this with sticky tape also. (diagram 9)

Open each of the 'cut' lines in this manner. Return the paper crown to the collar and secure at the C/F first. Stand back and look at the shape. (diagram 10)

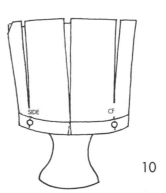

10

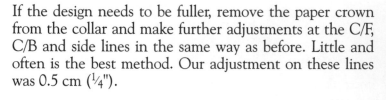

If the design needs to be fuller, remove the paper crown from the collar and make further adjustments at the C/F, C/B and side lines in the same way as before. Little and often is the best method. Our adjustment on these lines was 0.5 cm (¼").

11

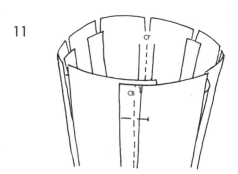

Remember to re-mark the C/F, C/B and sides

– these become notches which are very important when sewing the brim, peak, etc, to the side crown.

If adjustments have been made at the C/F, C/B and sides, mark halfway between the adjustments with a felt pen. These marks also become notch points and will help when attaching the side crown to the top crown and then to the brim. (diagram 11)

12

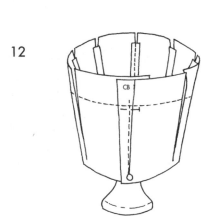

Stand back and look at the design. If the shape is right, now decide on the height of the crown. With a pencil, mark the desired height at the C/F, C/B and sides and then remove crown from collar. (diagram 12)

Lay the paper crown down.

13

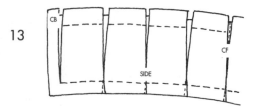

Measure, then mark the height of the crown from the collar edge. Be sure to mark the C/F, C/B and side at the collar edge and the top of side crown. (diagram 13)

TRANSFER TO PATTERN

Fold pattern paper of a suitable size in half. Place side crown pattern piece over pattern paper with C/F fold line in line with the folded edge of pattern paper, and secure with pins. As our design is symmetrical you can use either side of the crown. Some people work best from the left, others the right – do whatever is comfortable for you.

14

Trace the outline of the crown to pattern paper and then remove crown from paper. (diagram 14)

Unfold your pattern paper and check the folded line at C/F. This can sometimes have a dip up or down. Now is the time to smooth this into a nice rounded line at the top of the crown and at the collar edge.(diagram 15)

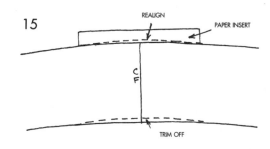

15

To avoid a dip up or down, square edge in from C/F edge by 0.75 cm (¼" to ⅜") at both the collar and top side crown edge.

Fold on C/F line again, secure pattern shape by pinning together with the design outline. Trace any alterations.

While the pattern paper is still folded, add seam allowances:

- 1.5 cm (⅝") at the collar edge
- 1 cm (⅜") at C/B seam
- 1 cm (⅜") at top of side crown. (diagram 16)

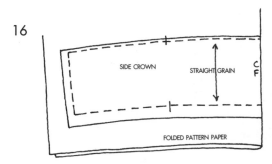

16

> When you become more experienced, you can use 0.5 cm (¼") seam allowance at top side crown. I prefer to sew the narrower seam.

THE STRAIGHT GRAIN

The straight grain of the side crown can be positioned to suit your design and the fabric pattern.

For a bias at the C/F, place a set square on the C/F line. Mark an equal distance on each edge of the set square. Draw a line connecting these marks. Write 'straight grain' along the line.

The straight grain can be parallel with C/F or on a bias across the C/F. (diagram 17)

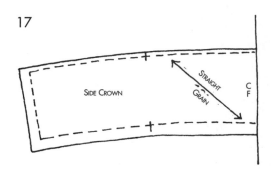

17

Now cut out your pattern with seam allowances and remember to mark notches. You now have a basic side crown pattern. Write design details on your paper pattern for easy identification – a small sketch of crown design, write 'side crown', size, cut 1 fabric, cut 1 Vilene, cut one wadding, and remember straight grain lines.

18

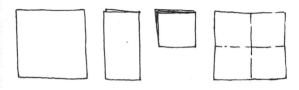

THE TOP CROWN

Fold a 25 cm (10") square of paper into quarters. Open out and rule a line on each crease line. (diagram 18)

Measure on the seam line at the top of the side crown, with the tape measure held upright, from the C/B to side 15.5 cm ($6\frac{1}{8}$"), to C/F 30.3 cm (12").

Note each measurement as you go. (diagram 19)

We have only measured half of the pattern piece.

19

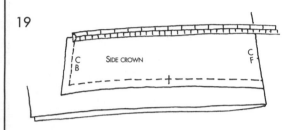

Unfold the paper. Lay collar on paper, aligning C/F, C/B and sides. Draw outline around collar edge. (diagram 20)

We double the top side crown measurement, so we are looking for 30.3 cm x 2 = 60.6 cm (24").

Our collar is 56 cm (22") so we have to enlarge the outline to 60.6 cm (24"). The way I do this is to measure out 1 cm ($\frac{3}{8}$") from the collar edge to begin with, all the way around the collar outline. (diagram 21)

Then with an upright tape measure, I measure on this line. Your measurements will vary, depending on the shape and size of the side crown. (diagram 22)

If the measurement is too big, make the measure from the collar edge outline a little less. If the measurement is too small, make the measure from the collar edge outline a little bigger. (The full circle method is illustrated in Chapter 3, 'The Top Beret'.)

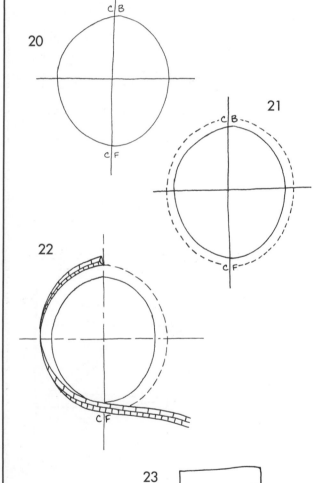

TRANSFER TO PATTERN

Fold pattern paper of a suitable size in half. On the folded edge of the pattern paper, place the folded top crown pattern on the C/F-C/B line – either side will do. Secure with pins.

Trace the outline and mark the side. Add a seam allowance of 1 cm ($\frac{3}{8}$"). As I mentioned before, I prefer 0.5 cm ($\frac{1}{4}$") but you decide which suits you from your own experience. (diagram 23)

THE STRAIGHT GRAIN

The straight grain of the top crown should be in line with what was decided for the side crown. The straight line that goes from C/F to C/B can be the straight grain line. For the bias, place a set square on the C/F-C/B line and mark an equal distance on each edge of the set square. Draw a line connecting these marks and write 'straight grain' along this line. (diagram 24)

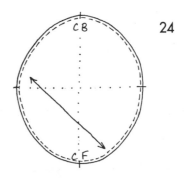

24

Cut out pattern and remember to mark notches for C/F, C/B and sides.

Write design details on the paper pattern for easy identification, e.g. a small sketch of crown design, write 'top crown', size, cut one fabric, cut one Vilene, cut one wadding, and remember straight grain lines.

See Chapter 8 for construction.

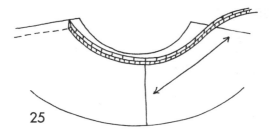

FITTING THE CROWN TO THE BRIM

When you join a crown to a brim it is important to measure from one C/B seam edge (with tape measure upright) around the collar edge seam line to the other C/B seam edge of each pattern piece. On folded pattern, C/B to side to C/F is fine. (diagrams 25 & 26)

25

If there is a variance in the measurement between the two, you need to make the necessary adjustments so that they fit one another.

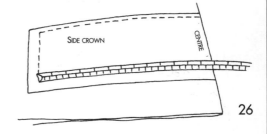

26

In our example, the adjustment was made to the brim collar edge. The crown measurement was slightly bigger. The unbroken line on the brim is the original brim and the broken line represents the new seam line and the amount trimmed from the collar edge of the brim pattern. (diagram 27)

The finished crown. (diagram 28)

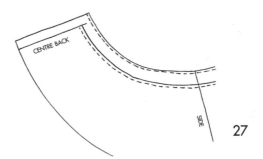

27

28

CHAPTER 3

THE BASIC BERET

After learning the technique for the basic brim you can now make a beret with a round top.

THE UNDER BERET

The under beret pattern can also be used as a brim pattern – it will fit close to the face and will turn up and stay up.

Fold a 45 cm (17¾") square of paper into quarters. Draw a line on the length of each fold line. (diagram 1)

Place the collar on the paper, aligning the marks on the collar with the lines on the paper. Draw a line around the collar and then remove it. (diagram 2)

Inside the collar line measure a 1.5 cm (⅝") seam allowance. On centre line mark C/F and C/B. (diagram 3)

Now decide the width of the beret.

In our example, the width is 11 cm (4¾"). From the collar line measure out 11 cm (4¼") all the way around (under beret width line). (diagram 4)

You now have the under beret outline. The following diagrams are specifically to do with the collar edge so the under beret outline has been omitted for the sake of space.

Cut out the inner section of the collar, leaving the seam allowance. (diagram 5)

Clip into the collar seam allowance to the collar line every 1 to 1.25 cm (⅜").

Clip either side of the C/F, C/B and side lines. These points are important when fitting the beret to a headband or a peak. Clip all the way around the collar seam allowance. (diagram 6)

Lift each clipped section and fold back onto the collar line, flatten them back, then lift them upright. (diagram 7)

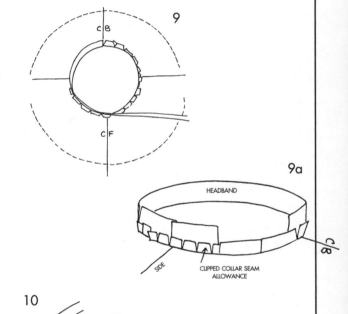

THE HEADBAND

Cut a strip of paper which is the length of the head measurement + 2 cm ($\frac{3}{4}$") for overlap x 3 cm ($1\frac{1}{4}$").

Fold the strip of paper lengthways, then in half end to end and the crease line becomes the C/F.

Our example is:
58 cm long x 3 cm wide ($22\frac{3}{4}$" long x $1\frac{1}{4}$" wide). (diagram 8)

Now unfold the headband and place one edge to the inside of the clipped edge of the collar seam allowance of the under beret draft. Pin the C/F crease in line with the C/F on the collar edge seam allowance and ease the headband around the edge to the C/B, overlapping the end of the headband 1 cm ($\frac{3}{8}$") on both sides. Secure with a pin at the C/B. Fold the headband over the upright clipped collar edge. (diagrams 9 & 9a)

With a needle and double thread, stitch the headband to the collar edge with a stab stitch, in and out, on an angle, to hold the two together. As you gain more experience you will be able to stick the headband to the collar with glue or staples but if this is your first time making a hat, please sew the headband to the collar. (diagrams 10 & 11)

Place the collar into the side beret headband, with C/F and C/B aligned. (diagram 12)

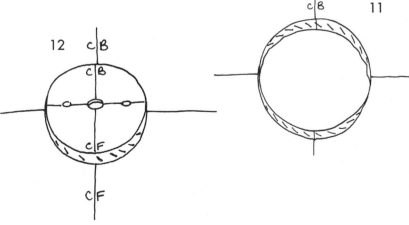

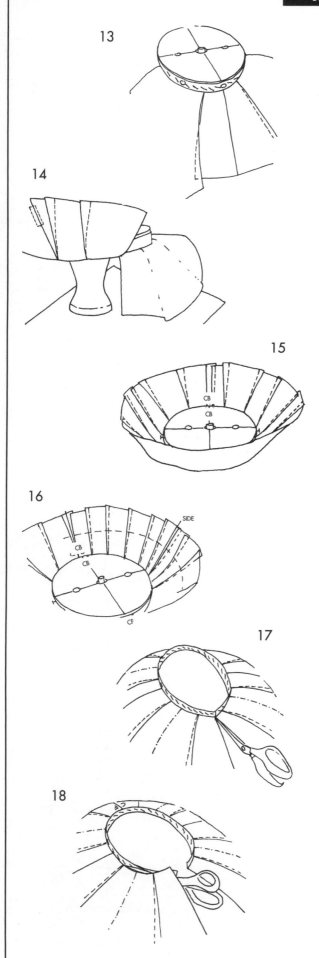

13

14

15

16

17

18

Secure with drawing pins at C/F, C/B and sides and place on stand. (diagram 13)

Now begin to shape your under beret.

Cut into the paper, between C/F and side line, from brim edge to collar edge. Overlap these by approximately 0.5 cm (¼") and secure with sticky tape at the side beret edge and collar edge, working up in the direction the under beret will sit. (diagram 14)

Work all the way around the side beret until it is the shape required.

> Remember it is best to overlap a little and often for the best results.

Stand back and look at the shape as you go. (diagram 15)

When the side beret looks the right shape, with a pencil lightly mark the height of the design on the inside.

Measure halfway between overlaps and C/F, C/B and sides on the outer edge of the under beret, and mark and draw a line down to the collar edge. These become notch marks. (diagram 16)

Remove the collar and under beret from the stand. Remove drawing pins and carefully lift the collar out of under beret headband.

Cut up C/B line and carefully cut around the collar line to remove the headband. (diagrams 17 & 18)

You now have an under beret pattern.

Define the collar line by redrawing the collar edge and smoothing out any dips or bumps. This now becomes the collar edge.

Make sure there are no dips or bumps.

This becomes the under beret pattern piece. (diagram 19)

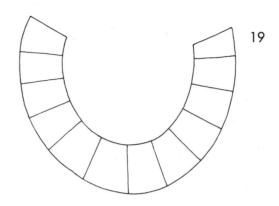

19

TRANSFER TO PATTERN

Fold pattern paper of a suitable size in half. Place under beret pattern piece over pattern paper, with C/F fold line in line with folded edge of pattern paper, and secure with pins. As our design is symmetrical, you can use either side of the under beret. Some people work best from the left, others the right – do whatever is comfortable for you. Transfer or trace the outline of the under beret to the pattern paper. (diagram 20)

Remove under beret from pattern paper.

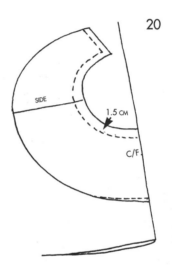

20

SIDE

1.5 CM

C/F

Unfold your pattern paper and check the folded line at C/F. This can sometimes have a dip up or down. Now is the time to smooth this into a rounded line at the top of the under beret and the collar edge.

To avoid a dip up or a dip down, 'square' edge in from the C/F edge by 0.75 cm (³⁄₈") at both the under beret and collar edge.

Fold on C/F line again and trace any alterations.

> Remember to mark notches and collar edge and brim edge.

While the pattern paper is still folded, add seam allowances:
• 1 cm (³⁄₈") at the collar edge
• 1 cm (³⁄₈") at C/B seam
• 1 cm (³⁄₈") at top under beret.

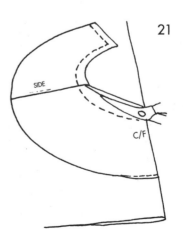

21

SIDE

C/F

I prefer a 0.5 cm (¹⁄₄") seam allowance at the top under beret because I find it easier to sew the two together. You decide which is best for you. Cut out the pattern piece with seam allowances. (diagram 21)

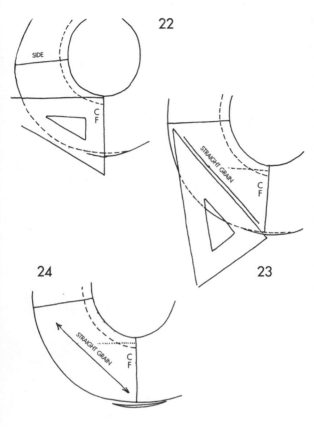

22

24

23

THE STRAIGHT GRAIN

This indicates the correct placement of pattern in line with straight weave of fabric. The straight grain of the under beret is generally parallel to the position where the beret is to stand upright – the C/F is appropriate, however, you can change this. It is up to you to decide which position is the most suited to your beret design and the fabric pattern.

For a bias at the C/F, place a set square on the C/F line. Mark an equal distance on each edge of the set square and draw a line connecting these marks and note both of these positions on your pattern. (diagrams 22 & 23)

Write 'straight grain' along the lines. The bias is now at the front of the under beret. (diagram 24)

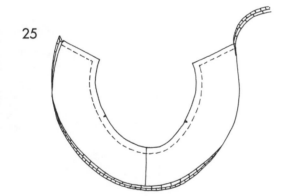

25

THE TOP BERET

Measure around the circumference of the top edge of the side beret and divide this by 3.14. (diagram 25)

In our example, the circumference of our top under beret edge is:

85 cm ÷ 3.14 = 27 ÷ 2 = 13.5 cm
($33\frac{1}{2}$" ÷ 3.14 = $10\frac{5}{8}$" ÷ 2 = $5\frac{3}{8}$").

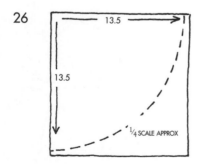

26

Now fold a 28 cm (11") square piece of paper into quarters. From the folded point measure out 13.5 cm ($5\frac{3}{8}$") along each folded edge, then from the folded point, from one folded edge to the other, measure out the 13.5 cm ($5\frac{3}{8}$") to create the curved edge. You now have a $\frac{1}{4}$ circle. (diagram 26)

Cut out and unfold and you have a circle to fit the top edge of your under beret.

If you want a more rounded edge to the top of the beret, increase the size of the circle, starting with 0.5 cm (¼") until it is right for your design.

This allows the top crown to curve slightly at the seam line. A snug fit can sometimes give the seam line a tight-looking edge but, as always, it depends on your design. (diagram 27)

THE STRAIGHT GRAIN

This indicates the correct placement of the pattern in line with the straight weave of the fabric. The straight grain of the top beret should run in the same direction as the under beret when the two are sewn together. Use the line C/F to C/B as one grain line, however, I find it useful to put all directions on my top crown. For the bias, place a set square on the C/F to C/B line. Mark an equal distance on each side of the set square and draw a line connecting these marks. (diagram 28)

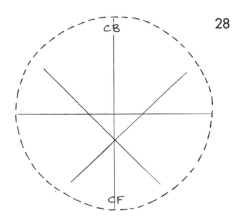

29

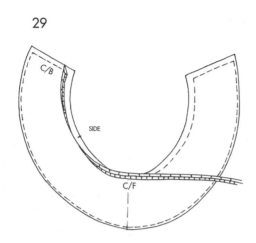

THE BANDEAU

The bandeau or headband prevents the collar edge from stretching.

Measure the length of the collar stitch line on the collar edge of the under beret. (diagram 29)

Then decide on the depth of the bandeau. If the finished depth is 3 cm ($1\frac{1}{8}$") you need to double this (because it is folded) and add a seam allowance of 3 cm ($1\frac{1}{8}$"):

3 cm x 2 = 6 cm + 2 cm seam allowance = 8 cm
($1\frac{1}{8}$" x 2 = $2\frac{3}{8}$" + $\frac{3}{4}$" seam allowance = $3\frac{1}{8}$")

Our example is:
56 cm + 2 cm = 58 cm length x 8 cm width
(22" + $\frac{3}{4}$" = $22\frac{3}{4}$ length x $3\frac{1}{8}$" width).

Onto pattern paper, measure and mark 58 cm ($22\frac{3}{4}$") length x 8 cm ($3\frac{1}{8}$") width.

Divide the length in half, 29 cm ($11\frac{1}{2}$"), and this becomes the C/F. Measure the distance between C/F and C/B and mark the side measurement to correspond with the collar edge measurement. (diagram 30)

30

C/F

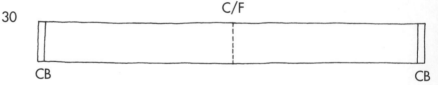

CB   CB

31

Now you can try out your pattern. Make a fabric toile to ensure that the pattern is right and to enable you to make any final design adjustments.

The finished beret. (diagram 31)

CHAPTER 4

THE BASIC PEAK

A peak can be used in a variety of combinations with crowns of all types.

Fold a 30 cm (12") square piece of paper into quarters. Draw a line the length of each fold line. (diagram 1)

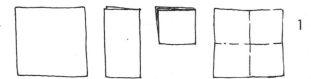

Place the collar on the paper, aligning the marks on the collar with the lines on the paper. Draw a line around the collar and remove the collar. (diagram 2)

Inside the collar line, measure 1.5 cm (⅝") seam allowance. On the centre line, mark C/F and C/B. (diagram 3)

Draw a rough pencil outline of the peak design wherever it is to be located. It can be at the front, back, to the side – it is up to you.

For this exercise it has been placed at the front. (diagram 4)

You now have the basic peak outline.

The following diagrams are specifically to do with the collar edge so the peak outline has been omitted for the sake of space.

Cut out the inner section of the collar, leaving the seam allowance. (diagram 5)

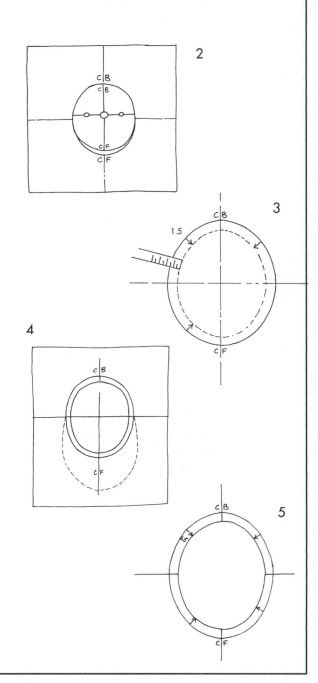

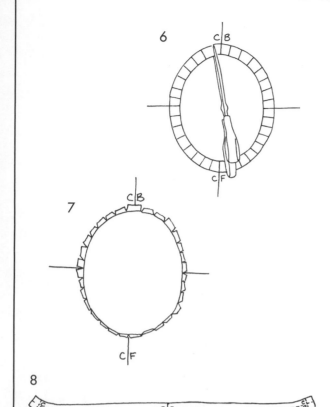

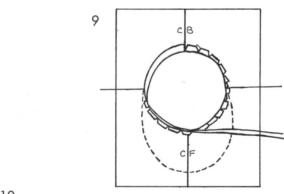

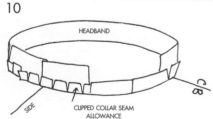

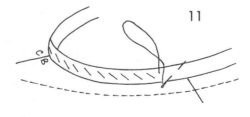

Clip into the collar seam allowance to the collar line every 1 to 1.25 cm (⅜"). Clip either side of the C/F, C/B and side lines (these points are important when fitting the peak to the crown).

Clip all the way around the collar seam allowance. (diagram 6)

Lift each clipped section and fold back onto the collar line, flatten them back, then lift them upright. (diagram 7)

THE HEADBAND

Cut a strip of paper the length of the head measurement + 2 cm (¾") for overlap x 3 cm (1⅛").

Now unfold the headband and place one edge to the inside of the clipped edge of the collar seam allowance on the peak draft. (diagram 8)

Pin the C/F crease in line with the C/F on the collar edge seam allowance and ease the headband around the edge to the C/B, overlapping the end of the headband 1 cm (⅜") either side and secure with a pin at C/B. Fold the headband over the upright clipped edge. (diagrams 9 & 10)

With a needle and double thread, stitch the headband to the collar edge with a stab stitch, in and out, on an angle, to hold the two together. (diagram 11)

As you gain more experience you will be able to stick the headband to the collar with glue or staples. If this is your first time making a hat, please sew the headband to the collar.

Our example is:

7 cm (2¾") to nothing at the side. (diagram 12)

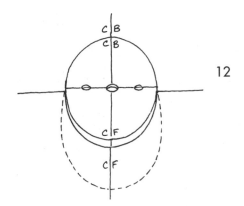

12

Place the collar into the headband with C/F and C/B aligned. Secure with drawing pins at C/F, C/B and the sides and place on the stand.

Now begin to design and shape your peak. Cut into the paper between C/F and side line, from peak edge to collar edge, overlapping by approximately 0.5 cm (¼"), securing with sticky tape at the peak and collar edge until the peak has the dip you want. Our example has two overlaps either side of C/F and one on the C/F.

If there is an overlap on the C/F, measure halfway between the overlap and mark and align to a 'new' C/F on the peak edge. Mark the position of C/F and sides at the collar edge.

These become the notch marks to use when fitting the peak to the crown etc. (diagram 13)

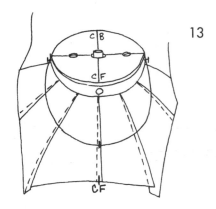

13

Remove collar and peak from stand.

Remove drawing pins and carefully lift collar out of headband.

Cut up C/B line and carefully cut around collar line to just beyond the C/F.

You only need to go a little past the C/F. I find it useful to keep the other side just in case I want a varied design for another project. (diagram 14)

If necessary, redraw the peak outline to smooth over any bumps or dips at the overlaps at the brim edge of the peak and collar edges.

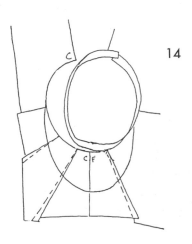

14

15

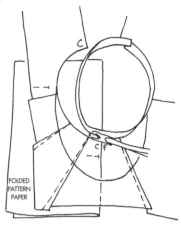

TRANSFER TO PATTERN

Fold pattern paper of a suitable size in half. Place peak pattern outline over pattern paper with C/F fold line in line with folded edge of pattern paper, and secure with pins. Transfer or trace the outline of the peak to the pattern paper. (diagram 15)

Remove the peak from pattern paper.

Unfold your pattern paper and check the folded line at C/F. This can sometimes have a dip up or down. Now is the time to smooth this into a rounded line at the collar edge and the brim edge of the peak.

To avoid a dip up and a dip down, 'square' edge in from the C/F edge by 0.75 cm ($\frac{1}{4}$" to $\frac{3}{8}$") at both the peak and collar edges.

Fold on C/F again and transfer or trace any alterations.

While the pattern paper is still folded, add seam allowances:

- 1 cm ($\frac{3}{8}$") at collar edge
- 0.5 cm ($\frac{1}{4}$") at peak edge. (diagram 16)

16

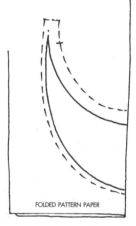

THE STRAIGHT GRAIN

This indicates the correct placement of the pattern in line with the straight weave of the fabric. The straight grain of the peak is generally parallel to C/F because this is the direction of the point of the peak. However, you can change this if you want. It is up to you to decide which position is the most suited to your design and fabric pattern.

For a bias at the C/F, place a set square on the C/F line and mark an equal distance on each edge of the set square. Draw a line connecting these marks and note both of these positions on your pattern. Write 'straight grain' along the lines. (diagram 17)

Now cut out your pattern with seam allowances.

17

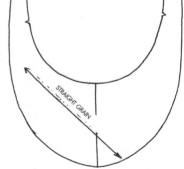

Remember the notches.

THE HEADBAND/BANDEAU

We need to make a bandeau to hold the peak to shape while trying on and for design purposes. Decide on finished depth of bandeau – then make a basic pattern.

18

Our example (finished bandeau) is:
56 cm long x 2.5 cm deep (22" x 1").

Onto pattern paper measure and mark the length of the head measurement 56 cm (22") + 2 cm (¾") seam allowance by the depth of the bandeau x 2 (because it is folded) + the collar edge seam allowance.

The finished depth is 2.5 cm (1") folded, so it is:
2.5 cm x 2 = 5 cm + 2 cm = 7 cm x 58 cm long
(1" x 2 = 2" + ¾" = 2¾" x 22¾"). (diagram 18)

MAKING A TOILE

19

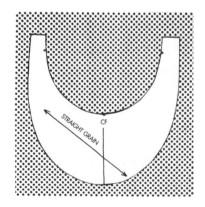

Cut one bandeau in fabric. Cut one peak in fabric and one peak in a medium-heavyweight Vilene, preferably iron-on. (diagram 19)

Bond the fabric and Vilene together.

To do this, lay the Vilene down on an ironing surface, adhesive side up. Then lay the fabric down over the Vilene, right side up. Ease the fabric to fit the Vilene, matching the notches. Lay a pressing cloth over peak and **press.** (diagram 20)

20

You can bond the fabric and Vilene together in one whole piece, then cut out your peak pattern.

21

Join the bandeau C/B seam. Remember 1 cm (³⁄₈") seam allowance at the collar edge for a peak.

It can be a little difficult to sew the straight bandeau to the curve of the peak collar edge, but if your measurements are correct, they will fit. Be patient, pin them together and carefully join the notches. Sew them together, slowly on the machine, with a long stitch length. (diagram 21)

22

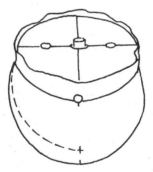

Clip the peak collar edge seam allowance to within 2 mm (¹⁄₁₆") of the stitch line. (diagram 22)

23

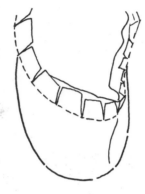

Place the collar back into the bandeau and peak, aligning the C/F and C/B. Secure with drawing pins and return to the stand.

Step back and look at the shape of your peak. (diagram 23)

24

Mark any alterations with a felt pen. It is a good idea to put it on a head, just to check the line and shape in relationship to the face. (diagram 24)

PLATE I

PLATE 2

PLATE 3

PLATE 4

Lay the pattern carefully over the fabric peak, brim edge to brim edge, and transfer the alterations to the paper pattern. (diagram 25)

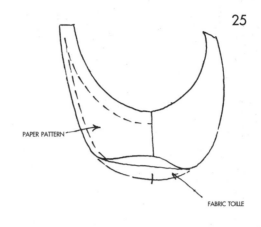

25

PAPER PATTERN

FABRIC TOILLE

You might prefer to place the fabric peak over the paper pattern. Do whatever you find is appropriate for your working method.

Remember to mark C/F and side notches and seam allowances on the new brim line of the peak.

I recommend that you transfer/trace to a new paper pattern piece – include the grain line and notches.

Peak attached to basic beret. (diagram 26)

26

A peak can be used in a variety of combinations with crowns of all types.

If the peak is to be attached to a bandeau, cut the bandeau to the head size. (diagram 27)

See Chapter 8 on construction for sewing your design.

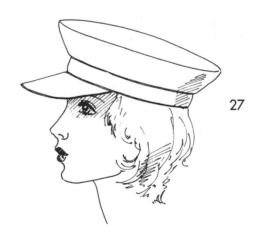

27

CHAPTER 5

CREATING YOUR OWN DESIGN

I recommend you make a basic hat, using the basic brim and crown method, before creating your own design.

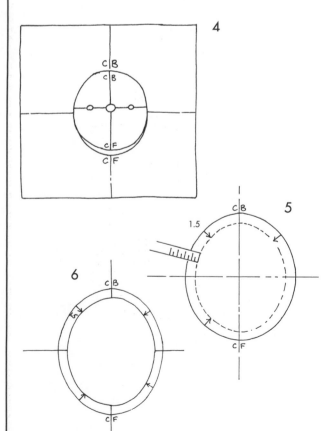

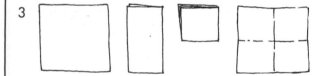

The example is for a large beret, worn to one side of the head.

In the illustration, the beret is worn to the right side but this could be changed to the left by just reversing the pattern (turning it over) when cutting out the fabric. (diagrams 1 & 2)

Decide on your design and take rough measurements of the dimensions – how wide you want it and how deep, etc.

In our example, the head measurement is 56 cm (22").

THE SIDE BERET

Fold a piece of paper of a suitable size for your design into quarters and draw a line on the length of each fold line. (diagram 3)

Place the collar on the paper, aligning the marks on the collar with the lines on the paper.

Draw a line around the collar and then remove the collar. (diagram 4)

Inside the collar line, measure in 1.5 cm ($\frac{5}{8}$") seam allowance. On centre line mark C/F and C/B. (diagram 5)

Cut out the inner section of the collar, leaving the seam allowance. (diagram 6)

Clip into the collar seam allowance to the collar line every 1 to 1.25 cm (⅝"). Clip either side of the C/F, C/B and side lines. These points are important when fitting the beret to the headband.

Clip all the way around the collar seam allowance. (diagram 7)

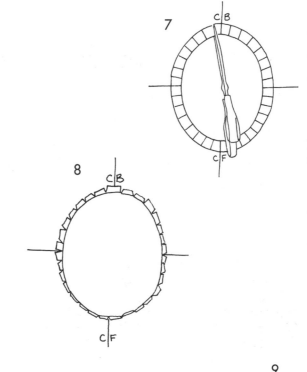

Lift each clipped section and fold back onto the collar line, flatten them back, then lift them upright. (diagram 8)

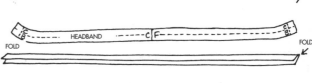

THE HEADBAND

Cut a strip of paper which is the length of the head measurement + 2 cm (¾") for overlap x 3 cm (1⅛").

Fold the strip in half lengthways, then in half crossways. The crease line becomes the C/F.

Our example is:
58 cm long x 3 cm wide (22¾" long x 1⅛" wide). (diagram 9)

Unfold the headband and place one edge to the inside of the clipped edge of the collar seam allowance. Pin the C/F crease in line with the C/F on the collar edge seam allowance and ease the headband around the edge to the C/B, overlapping the end of the headband 1 cm (⅜") either side. Secure with a pin at the C/B. Fold the headband over the upright clipped collar edge. (diagrams 10 & 11)

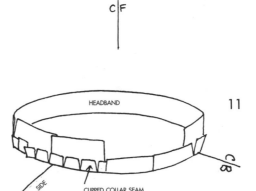

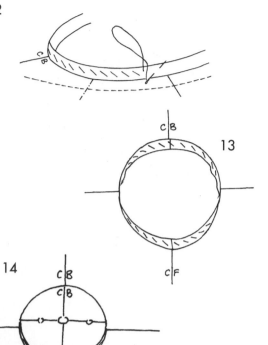

12

With a needle threaded double, stitch the headband to the collar edge with a stab stitch, in and out, on an angle, to hold the two together. (diagrams 12 & 13)

As you gain more experience, you will be able to stick the headband to the collar with either glue or staples.

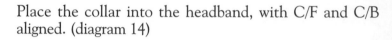

13

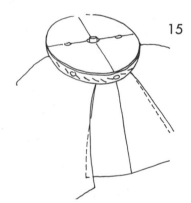

14

Place the collar into the headband, with C/F and C/B aligned. (diagram 14)

15

Secure with drawing pins at C/F, C/B and sides. Place on the stand. (diagram 15)

Now begin to create and shape your design.

16

As with the basic brim, cut from the outside edge into the collar edge, overlapping and sticking little and often. In the case of this beret, we need to insert paper to increase the underside (right) of the beret design.

Our example is upright on the left side so the overlap at this point is wider – getting smaller towards the front and the back.

The right side has added fullness in the first cut to the right from the C/F because of the drape to that side. (diagram 16)

Where you need to **take out** fullness, overlap the cuts into the beret as much and as often as needed to create the required shape, securing each with sticky tape.

Where you need to **put in** fullness, open the cuts into the beret as much and as often as needed to create the required shape, inserting paper and securing with sticky tape.

The cut to right side of C/F (left side in diagram) in this example is opened 9 cm (3½") and a piece of paper inserted and held in place with sticky tape. The next cut towards the side is opened 2 cm (¾") and a piece of paper inserted and held in place with tape.

As we continue towards the left, the cuts are overlapped, the first 6 cm (2⅜"), the next 3 cm (1⅛"). (diagram 17)

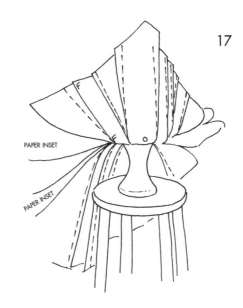

17

Make sure the sticky tape is holding your adjustments securely.

Stand back and look at your design, making any necessary adjustments to create the shape required. Now draw the outline of your design onto the paper beret and be sure to mark C/F, C/B and side lines. If there are overlaps or inserts at these points, measure and mark half the distance between them to enable you to relocate the notch points, and lightly mark down to the collar edge. (diagram 18)

Remove the collar with paper beret from the stand. **Carefully** remove the collar from the headband of the paper beret.

Cut up the C/B seam and carefully cut off the headband.

Lay the paper beret shape flat and **gently** press down any bumps in the paper.

Redraw your outline at the collar edge and the outside side beret edge, smoothing out any bumps and dips that may have resulted at the overlaps and inserts. Define a clear outer edge with a good shape. (diagram 19)

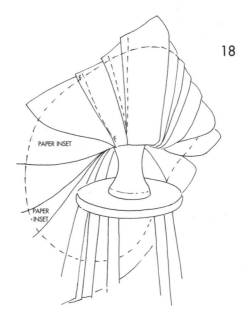

18

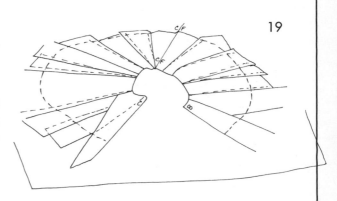

19

20

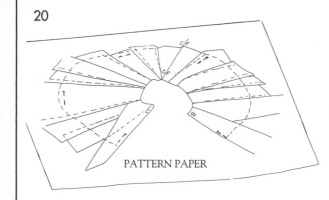

PATTERN PAPER

TRANSFER TO PATTERN

Pin your design onto pattern paper of a suitable size and secure with pins.

Transfer/trace the design outline onto the pattern paper and mark C/F, C/B and sides at the collar edge and the beret edge. These will be the notch points.

> Remember to mark the notches.

It is also useful to rule a line to connect these notch points across the pattern. (diagram 20)

Remove the paper beret from the pattern paper.

Add seam allowances:

- 1 cm (⅜") to collar edge
- 1 cm (⅜") to back seam
- 0.5 cm (¼") to beret edge.

Cut out paper pattern. (diagram 21)

21

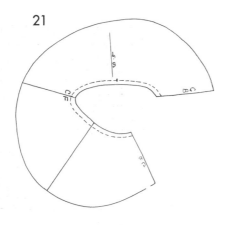

THE STRAIGHT GRAIN

Because the design is upright on the left in our example, the straight grain is parallel with the left side line that runs from the collar edge to the brim edge.

THE BANDEAU

We need to know the side beret collar edge measurement for the bandeau.

22

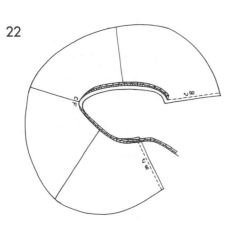

With the tape measure held upright on the stitch line on the collar edge, from C/B seam edge measure to the side, to C/F, to the side, back to the other C/B seam edge. Record each section measurement on the pattern as you go. (diagram 22)

Cut a paper pattern to these measurements and be sure to note and mark the side and C/F measurements adding 1 cm (⅜") seam allowance at each end for the C/B seam x the width of the headband x 2 + 2 cm (¾") seam allowance for attachment to the collar edge.

In our example, the finished width of the bandeau is 2.5 cm (1"). The measurements to correspond with the collar seam line are:

23

- C/B to right side 15.5 cm (6⅛")
- Right side to C/F 29 cm (11½")
- C/F to left side 45 cm (17¾")
- Left side to C/B 57 cm (22½").
  (diagram 23)

So the dimensions of our paper pattern are:

- 57 cm length + 2 cm seam allowance = 59 cm (22½" + ¾" seam allowance = 23¼").

- 2.5 cm width x 2 = 5 cm + 2 cm seam allowance = 7 cm (1" x 2 = 2" + ¾" seam allowance = 2¾").

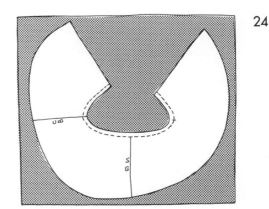

24

MAKING A TOILE

Cut one beret pattern in fabric and one in medium weight Vilene (preferably iron-on/fusible). (diagram 24)

Remember to mark the notches.

It is a good idea to do a test – pressing a piece of the fabric to the Vilene. Some fashion fabrics need a pressing cloth.

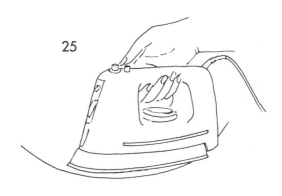

25

Bond the two together – the fabric pattern has a bias edge, so handle carefully to avoid stretching out of shape. Lay the Vilene pattern down, adhesive side up, on an ironing surface large enough to accommodate the whole pattern. Lay the fabric pattern down over the Vilene, right side up. Ease the fabric piece to fit the Vilene, matching notches, and **press** with the iron. (diagram 25)

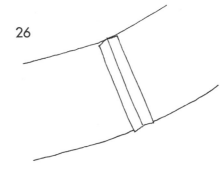

26

Cut one bandeau in fabric and remember to mark the notches.

Sew the C/B seam of the beret and the bandeau and press the seams open. (diagram 26)

27

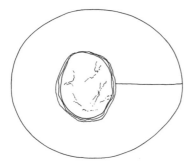

Pin the bandeau to the side beret at the collar edge, joining at the notches first, then easing one to fit the other.

Remember that the bandeau is on the straight grain of the fabric and collar edge is more of a bias. If your measurements are correct, they will fit – just be patient. Machine stitch together with a long machine stitch. (diagram 27)

28

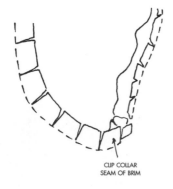

CLIP COLLAR
SEAM OF BRIM

Clip, on a slight angle, into the collar edge seam allowance to within 2 to 3 mm ($^1/_{16}$") of machine stitching. (diagram 28)

Do not cut the bandeau.

Fold the bandeau over to encase the clipped collar edge and machine stitch together using a long machine stitch – it is easier to unpick if alterations are necessary.

29

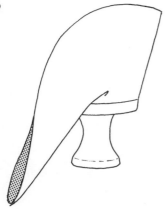

Now place the collar into the headband of the beret, aligning C/F and C/B and secure with drawing pins. Place collar on stand. (diagram 29)

Stand back and look at the shape of your design.

30

Better still, place it on a head to have a better perspective of the shape in relation to the face and body. Look at the shape and be sure it looks 'balanced' from all angles. (diagram 30)

With a felt pen, mark any alterations. Eliminate any unwanted fullness by pinning darts in the appropriate places. If you need to extend the outer edge, pin a piece of Vilene to the edge and redraw the outline. (diagram 31)

RELOCATING A SEAM

In the example, the seam at C/B was relocated to the right side so that the seam would not be visible.

With a felt pen, mark the new position of the seam line on the toile. Here, the new position is on the right side.

Remove the toile from the stand and collar and make sure all alterations are clearly marked. Carefully unpick the stitching – this is why a long machine stitch is used – and remove the headband.

Lay the fabric beret pattern down over the paper pattern. Transfer and mark any alterations from the fabric to the paper pattern.

If the outline has been enlarged, pin a piece of paper at the appropriate place on the pattern. (diagram 32)

On the paper pattern, draw a line where the new seam line is to be. In our example, this is the right side mark. (diagram 33)

Cut up this line from beret edge to collar edge. (diagram 34)

Carefully overlap the C/B seam allowance, aligning the stitch lines over each other. You now have an opening at the right side. (diagram 35)

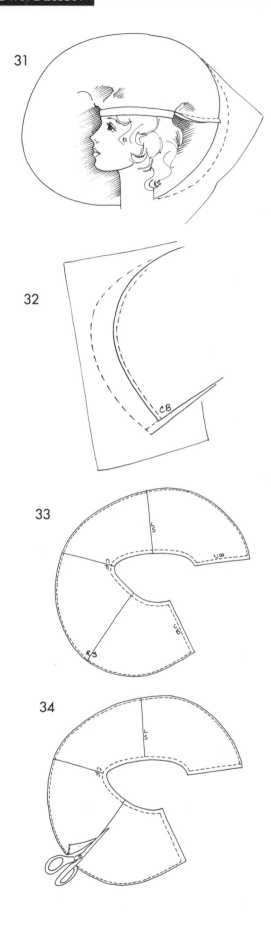

31

32

33

34

35

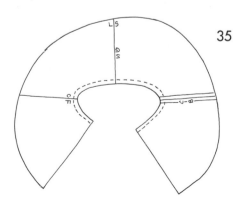

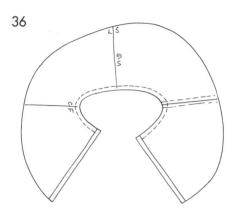

36

Glue paper to either side for new seam allowance. Now you must add 1 cm (³⁄₈") seam allowance from the cut edge out on the paper insert. (diagram 36)

Redraw the outline of the pattern smoothing over any dips or bumps. Take particular notice of the overlap at the C/B – make sure this has a nice line.

If the pattern is looking a bit untidy, trace the new outline to a fresh piece of pattern paper. Cut out the paper pattern.

Remember to transfer all the notches.

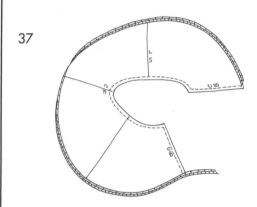

37

THE TOP BERET

If the top of your beret is a circle, with tape measure upright, measure around the circumference of the top edge of the side beret, divide this by 3.14.

In our example, the circumference of our top edge is:

142.7 cm ÷ 3.14 = 45.4 cm ÷ 2 = 22.7 cm
(56¹⁄₁₆" ÷ 3.14 = 17⁷⁄₈" ÷ 2 = 9") (diagram 37)

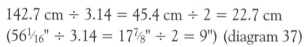

38

Now fold a 50 cm (19³⁄₄") square piece of paper into quarters. From the folded point, measure out 23.7 cm (9³⁄₈") along each folded edge. Then, from the folded point from one folded edge to the other, measure out the 23.7 cm (9³⁄₈") to create a curved edge. You have made a ¹⁄₄ circle. (diagram 38)

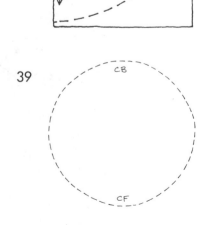

39

Cut out and unfold. You now have a circle to fit the outside edge of your side beret (including seam allowance). (diagram 39)

THE STRAIGHT GRAIN

This should correspond and run down from the point where the straight grain line is on the side beret. In our example, the straight grain is from the left side notch.

With the tape measure held upright, start on a section of the circle where the straight weave of the fabric is where the left notch will be located. Measure an equal distance to C/F to right side, and then to C/B to right side to correspond with the measurements on the side beret.

If you want a fuller edge to the top of the beret, increase the size of the circle, starting with 0.5 cm (¼") and adjusting until it is just right for your design. (diagram 40)

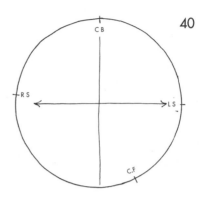

AN ASYMMETRICAL SHAPE

If your beret design is asymmetrical or an unusual shape, you will need to make another toile, and create a top beret to fit your side beret.

Cut and assemble the side beret as described in 'Making a Toile' on page 39. Place the collar in the bandeau and place on the stand.

Pin a large piece of plain Vilene onto and around the side beret, allowing fullness for the head. With a felt pen, draw an outline of the side beret shape onto the Vilene, marking the C/F, C/B and left side. Double notch left side. (diagram 41)

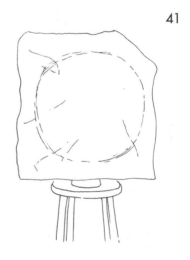

Place the toile on a head to view the overall look of the design in proportion to the face. (diagrams 42 & 43)

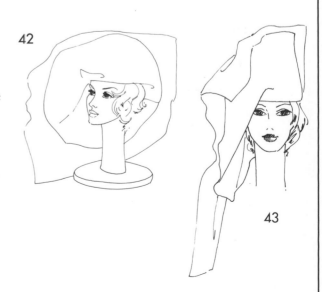

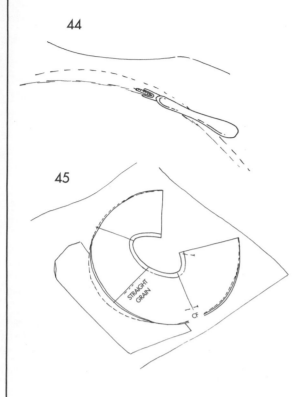

44

45

Remove the Vilene outline. Trace this outline onto pattern paper.

> Remember to mark C/F, C/B and left side.

Add a 0.5 cm (¼") seam allowance. (diagram 44)

Trace the alterations to the side beret. (diagram 45)

TRANSFER TO PATTERN

Pin your design onto pattern paper of a suitable size and secure with pins. Trace the design outline to the pattern paper. Mark C/F, C/B and left side notches – double notch for left side – at the top beret edge.

THE STRAIGHT GRAIN

This indicates the correct placement of pattern in line with the straight weave of the fabric. Remember, the design stands upright on the left side so it's necessary to have the straight grain line drawn straight down from the left side notches.

Reassemble the side beret as described in 'Making the toile'. The top beret is cut and assembled in the same manner as the side beret. Sew the back seam of the side beret, then sew the top beret to the side beret, taking care to align the notches.

Make any adjustments to the design and transfer these to the paper pattern.

When your pattern is completed, write the relevant information and a sketch on the pattern pieces for future reference. Also put 'RSU' (right side up) so that if you decide to make the beret in reverse, you'll have this easy reference when laying pattern pieces on fabric. The 'RSU' won't show.

Now it is up to you to create your own design.

CHAPTER 6

PIECE CROWNS

Piece crowns can be used in a variety of styles like a three-piece sports cap, (diagrams 1 & 1a) or a fitted six-piece schoolboy's cap. (diagrams 2 & 2a)

Three-, four-, five-, and six-piece styles

1

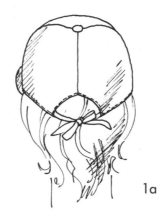

1a

2

2a

3

You can have as many 'pieces' in a crown as suits your design. More than six pieces though, does get a little fiddly but it can be done. Simply divide the head measurement by the number of pieces in the crown.

The basic measurements required are:

- Head measurement 56 cm (22")
- Ear-to-ear measurement 34 cm (13½")
- Front-to-back measurement 36 cm (14⅛")

3a

A variety of brims can be used with any number of piece crown designs. Diagrams 3 and 3a are an example of a 'full' top crown with a slightly sloping brim that can be comfortably worn up on one side. Diagrams 4 and 4a have a rounded top crown with a more sloping, face-hugging brim which easily turns up all the way around.

So, in our example:

for a three-piece –
56 cm (22") ÷ 3 = 18.6 cm (7⅜")
one crown piece is ⅓ head measurement

4

for a four-piece –
56 cm (22") ÷ 4 = 14 cm (5½")
one crown piece is ¼ head measurement

for a five-piece –
56 cm (22") ÷ 5 = 11.2 cm (4⅜")
one crown piece is ⅕ head measurement

for a six-piece –
56 cm (22") ÷ 6 = 9.3 cm (3⅝")
one crown piece is ⅙ head measurement.

Then, we divide the ear-to-ear measurement by 2.

So, in our example 34 cm (13½") ÷ 2 = 17 cm (6⅜").

4a

The dimension for each piece design is approximately a rectangle shape of half the ear-to-ear measurement x crown piece.

THE THREE-PIECE CROWN

Draw a rectangle for one crown piece with the following dimensions:
18.6 cm (7⅜") x 17 cm (6¾").

Divide this in half lengthways:
18.6 cm (7⅜") ÷ 2 = 9.3 cm (3⅝").

From the top of the centre line, measure down 4 cm (1⅝") and square a line across. Then measure down another 4 cm (1⅝") and square a line across. We have moved down a total of 8 cm (3⅛"). (diagram 5)

Now you shape the crown.

For a fuller top, you should follow the broken line, and for a flatter top, follow the unbroken line. (diagram 6)

If your crown is to sit at an angle on the head make a toile of a three-piece crown.

Fit the toile to the head and mark with a felt tip pen the line of the crown edge. Measure and adjust the collar edge to fit the brim, headband or peak.

Add a seam allowance of 1 cm (⅜") to the side seams.

Add the seam allowance to the collar edge after you have decided on the design and depth of your crown – usually 1.5 cm (⅝") if the crown is to be attached to a brim or 1 cm (⅜") if it is to be attached to a headband or a peak.

Mark a notch on the second line from the top of the peak – this can be very useful when matching stripes and checks.

Write the design description and draw an illustration of the design on each pattern piece. Include size, and instructions such as 'cut 3 fabric', 'cut 3 Vilene', 'cut 3 wadding'.

STRAIGHT GRAIN

See 'General Hints', page 52.

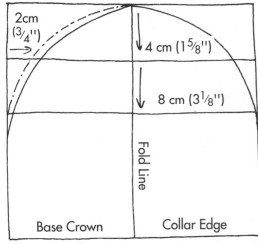

5

↓ 4 cm (1⅝")

↓ 8 cm (3⅛")

Fold line

Base Crown   Collar Edge

⅓ head measurement
18.6 cm (7⅜")

6

2cm (¾")→

↓ 4 cm (1⅝")

↓ 8 cm (3⅛")

Fold Line

Base Crown   Collar Edge

⅓ head measurement
18.6 cm (7⅜")

Diagram 7

7

Top Crown

2 cm (¾") | 3.5 cm (1⅜")

Fold Line

9.5 cm (3¼")

Base Crown | Collar Edge

¼ head measurement
14 cm (5½")

Diagram 8

8

Top Crown

2 cm (¾") | 3.5 cm (1⅜")

Fold Line

9.5 cm (3¼")

Base Crown | Collar Edge

¼ head measurement
14 cm (5½")

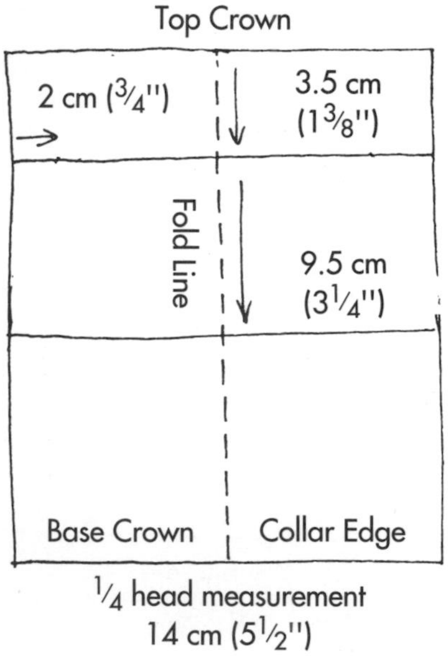

THE FOUR-PIECE CROWN

Draw a rectangle for one crown piece with the following dimensions:
14 cm (5½") x 17 cm (6¾").

Divide the rectangle in half lengthways:
14 cm (5½") ÷ 2 = 7 cm (2¾").

From the top of the centre line, measure down 3.5 cm (1⅜") and square a line across. Measure down another 6 cm (2⅜") and square a line across. We have now moved down a total of 9.5 cm (3¾"). (diagram 7)

Now you shape the crown.

For a fuller top, you should follow the broken line and for a flatter top, follow the unbroken line. (diagram 8)

If your crown is to sit at an angle on the head, make a toile of a four-piece crown.

Fit the toile to the head and mark with a felt tip pen the line of the crown edge. Measure and adjust the collar edge to fit the brim, headband or peak.

Add a seam allowance of 1 cm (⅜") to the side seams.

Add the seam allowance to the collar edge after you have decided on the design and depth of your crown – usually 1.5 cm (⅝") if the crown is to be attached to a brim, or 1 cm (⅜") if it is to be attached to a headband or a peak.

Mark a notch on the second line from the top of the peak – this can be very useful when matching stripes and checks.

Write the design description and draw an illustration of the design on each pattern piece. Include size, and instructions such as 'cut 4 fabric', 'cut 4 Vilene', 'cut 4 wadding'.

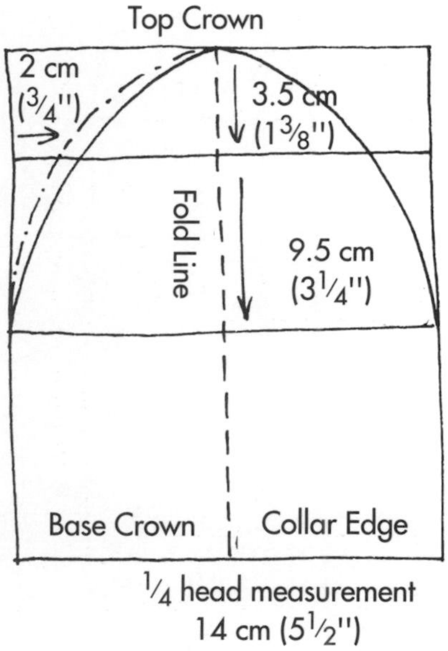

STRAIGHT GRAIN

See 'General Hints', page 52.

THE FIVE-PIECE CROWN

Draw a rectangle for one crown piece with the following dimensions:
11.2 cm (4⅜") x 17 cm (6¾").

Divide the rectangle in half lengthways:
11.2 cm (4⅜") ÷ 2 = 5.6 cm (2¼").

From the top of the centre line, measure down 2.5 cm (1") and square a line across. Measure down 7 cm (2¾") and square a line across. We have now moved down a total of 9 cm (3½"). (diagram 9)

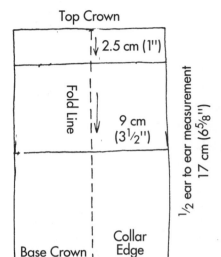

Now you shape the crown.

For a fuller top you should follow the broken line and for a flatter top, follow the unbroken line. (diagram 10)

If your crown is to sit at an angle on the head, make a toile of a five-piece crown.

Fit the toile to the head and mark with a felt tip pen the line of the crown edge. Measure and adjust the collar edge to fit the brim, headband or peak.

Add a seam allowance of 1 cm (⅜") to the side seams.

Add the seam allowance to the collar edge after you have decided on the design and depth of your crown – usually 1.5 cm (⅝") if the crown is to be attached to a brim or 1 cm (⅜") if it is to be attached to a headband or a peak.

Mark a notch on the second line from the top of the peak – this can be very useful when matching stripes and checks.

Write the design description and draw an illustration of the design on each pattern piece. Include size, and instructions such as 'cut 5 fabric', 'cut 5 Vilene', 'cut 5 wadding'.

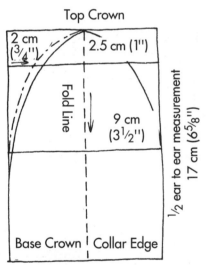

STRAIGHT GRAIN

See 'General Hints,' page 52.

11

Top Crown

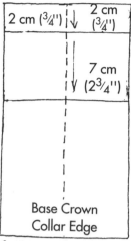

2 cm (¾") 2 cm (¾")

7 cm (2¾")

Base Crown
Collar Edge

⅙ head measurement
9.3 cm (3⅝")

THE SIX-PIECE CROWN

Draw a rectangle for one crown piece with the following dimensions:
9.3 cm (3⅗") x 17 cm (6¾").

Divide the rectangle in half lengthways:
9.3 cm (3⅝") ÷ 2 = 4.6 cm (1⅝").

From the top of the centre line, measure down 2 cm (¾") and square a line across. Measure down another 5 cm (2") and square a line across. We have now moved down 7 cm (2¾"). (diagram 11)

Now you shape the crown. For a fuller top, you should follow the broken line, and for a flatter top, follow the unbroken line. (diagram 12)

If your crown is to sit at an angle on the head, make a toile of a six-piece crown. Fit the toile to the head and mark the line of the crown edge with a felt tip pen. Measure and adjust the collar edge to fit the brim, head-band or peak.

Add a seam allowance of 1 cm (⅜") to the side seams.

Add the seam allowance to the collar edge after you have decided on the design and depth of your crown – usually 1.5 cm (⅝") if the crown is to be attached to a brim or 1 cm (⅜") if it is to be attached to a headband or a peak.

Mark a notch on the second line from the top of the peak – this can be very useful when matching stripes and checks.

Write the design description and draw an illustration of the design on each pattern piece. Include size, and instructions such as 'cut 6 fabric', 'cut 6 Vilene', 'cut 6 wadding'.

12

Top Crown

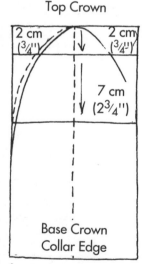

2 cm (¾") 2 cm (¾")

7 cm (2¾")

Base Crown
Collar Edge

⅙ head measurement
9.3 cm (3⅝")

STRAIGHT GRAIN

See 'General Hints' on page 52.

THE BERET

The 'piece' design principle is used for both a fuller blouson-style beret and a close-fitting beret.

For a blouson style, lengthen the pattern piece and alter the width at the appropriate point above the collar edge.

Never alter the base crown width of your pattern.

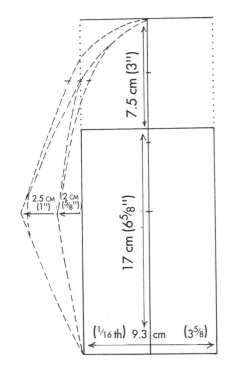

13

Start with a rectangle for a crown. To this add the height and width appropriate for the design.

In diagram 13, 7.5 cm (3") has been added to the height of the rectangle.

At approximately 10 cm (4") from the base crown, width has been added to create the blouson effect. You only need to work on one side of the rectangle.

In diagram 14, 2 cm (¾") has been added

In diagram 15, 4.5 cm (1¾") has been added.

When the design looks in proportion, add seam allowances, then fold the rectangle in half and cut out the pattern outline.

Remember to mark the notches.

14

15

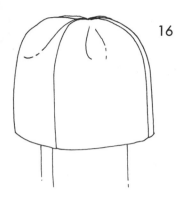

16

17

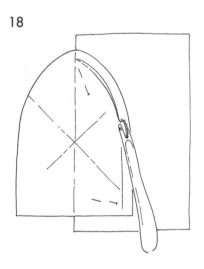

18

GENERAL HINTS FOR 'PIECE' CROWN DESIGNS

In the shaping diagrams, the unbroken line is for a flatter, rounded style and the broken line for a fuller look.

Make up a toile of your design and sew it with a long machine stitch, for easy unpicking for any alterations that may be necessary.

Place your piece crown on the collar and stand back and look at the shape. (diagram 16)

If the top of the crown is too full, pin out the fullness. (diagram 17)

Transfer alterations on the fabric pattern to a folded piece of pattern paper and do not forget to transfer notches. (diagram 18)

I find it useful to cut my piece patterns in firm, transparent plastic or perspex. This is handy if you are matching stripes or checks.

THE STRAIGHT GRAIN

This refers to the placement of the pattern in line with the straight weave of the fabric and, on piece crowns, it is useful to have the straight grain down the centre of the pattern piece.

Locate the bias going in two directions. To position the bias on your pattern piece, place a set square on the centre line of the pattern. Mark an equal distance on each side of the square and draw a line connecting these marks as shown in diagram 18.

CHAPTER 7

THE THREE-PIECE 'ROUND' CROWN

This style of crown is very useful because it is easily modified for different designs. These hats have a panel going from C/F to C/B (top crown) with rounded side crowns.

The basic three-piece round crown can be used with the basic brim, (diagram 1) or the basic peak. (diagram 2)

In diagram 3, 2.5 cm (1") has been added to the height of the crown and attached to the basic brim.

In our example the:
• Head measurement is 56 cm (22")
• Ear-to-ear measurement is 34 cm (13⅜")
• Front-to-back measurement is 36 cm (14⅛").

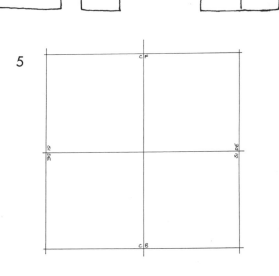

> If the ear-to-ear and front-to-back measurements are different, use the greater measurement.

Fold a 38 cm (15") square piece of paper into quarters. Unfold the paper and rule a line along each fold line. (diagram 4)

From the centre, along each line, measure out 18 cm (7⅛") and mark this square. At each end of one of these lines write 'side', and mark C/F and C/B on the ends of the other line. (diagram 5)

6

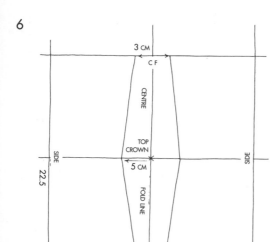

Decide on the width of the centre panel top crown, at the C/F and the C/B and across the top of the head.

Our example is:
- centre front 6 cm (2⅜")
- centre back 5 cm (2"). (diagram 6)

Add these two measurements together and subtract them from the head measurement:
56 cm – 11 cm = 45 cm (22" – 4⅜" = 17¾").

We then divide this by two, because we have two side crowns.

Each side crown is 22.5 cm (8⅞") at the collar edge.

7

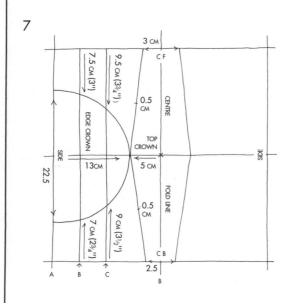

We measure 11.25 cm (4½") either side of the ruled side line.

Measure and draw a line halfway between line A and line C. This is line D. Now:
- from the 'back' on line C measure in 9 cm (3½")
- from the 'back' on line D measure in 7 cm (2¾")
- from the 'front' on line C measure in 9.5 cm (3¾")
- from the 'front' on line D measure in 7.5 cm (3").

Now for the *side crown*. Draw an arched line connecting the back edge of the side crown to the edge of the top crown around to the front edge of the side crown.

Use the measurement marks on lines C and D at front and back to create the 'curved' edge of the side crown. (diagram 7)

8

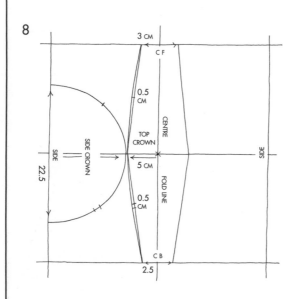

For the *top crown*, we measure out from the centre of the top panel 5 cm (2") either side for the top width of the top crown.

Our example is 10 cm (4").

From this point, rule a line connecting C/F to C/B. On each of these lines, measure and mark halfway from C/F and C/B to top. On these marks, measure out 0.5 cm (¼"). Draw a curved line connecting C/F to C/B. (diagram 8)

9

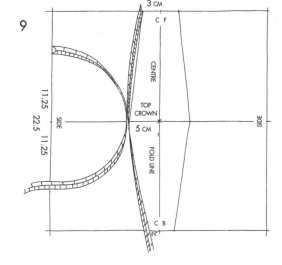

Holding the tape measure upright along the side of the top crown, measure halfway from the back to the top and mark. Then measure halfway from the front to the top and mark. Notch once at the front and 0.5 cm (¼") either side of the back mark. (diagram 9)

Do the same measurement on the curved edge of the side crown. (diagram 9a) These notches make the sewing construction easier.

TRANSFER TO PATTERN

This follows the general method used for the other basic designs.

9a

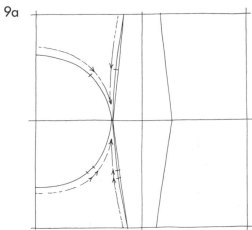

For the top crown, fold paper of a suitable size in half. Place the draft of the top crown on the paper with the centre top crown line on the edge of the fold, and trace the top crown outline. Be sure to mark notches at front, back and centre top.

Remove draft and unfold for final pattern outline. (diagram 10)

Add seam allowances:

• 1 cm (⅜") on seams
• 1.5 cm (⅝") to collar edge if joining to brim
• 1 cm (⅜") to collar edge if joining to a peak.

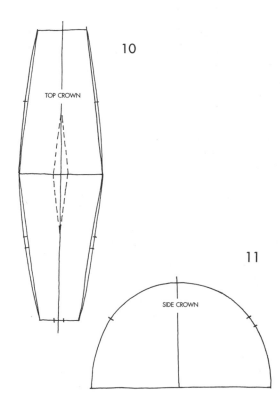

For the side crown, lay the draft over a suitably sized piece of paper and trace the side crown outline.

Be sure to mark the notches at front, back and centre top.

Remove draft for the final pattern outline. (diagram 11)

THE STRAIGHT GRAIN

This indicates the correct placement of the pattern in line with the straight weave of the fabric.

It is optional where you put the straight grain. In a three-piece round crown the fabric design can determine how the pattern pieces are placed. I mark all options on my pattern pieces.

On the top crown, I have the straight grain on the centre line going from C/F to C/B. (diagram 12)

For a bias, I place a set square on the straight grain line and mark an equal distance on each edge of the set square and draw a line connecting these marks. I have a bias going in the other direction as well.

On the side crown, I have the straight grain along the side line from the collar edge to the top edge. I use the same method for the bias as I do with the top crown. (diagram 13)

12

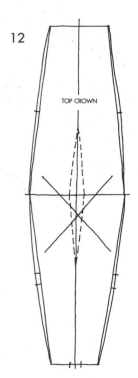

TOP CROWN

13

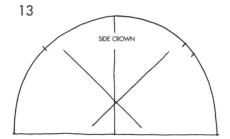

SIDE CROWN

PLATE 5

PLATE 6

PLATE 7

PLATE 8

CHAPTER 8

CONSTRUCTION

In this chapter we learn how to construct the basic crown, brim and beret.

In chapter 11 you will find full-size pattern pieces in five sizes. The larger pattern pieces are spread over two pages so it will be necessary to join the patterns on the respective broken lines.

TRANSFERRING THE PATTERNS

MATERIALS AND EQUIPMENT
- Tracing paper
- Pencil
- Scissors

Fold a piece of 45 cm (18") square piece of tracing paper in half and crease on the fold.

Lay the folded edge of the tracing paper in line with the C/F fold line on the front section of the pattern piece. With a pencil draw around the pattern outline. Include the broken line 'join pattern piece here', centre front fold and the straight grain line.

Overlay the front section over the back section at the 'join pattern piece here' and trace back section onto the tracing paper. (diagram 1)

Turn the tracing over and trace the outline to the other side of the paper.

Unfold the tracing and make sure theC/F edge is rounded at the brim and collar edge. You now have a complete outline of the pattern piece.

Cut out the pattern piece. (diagram 2)

It is a good idea to transfer the pattern outline to a firmer piece of paper or light card.

Remember to clip the notches.

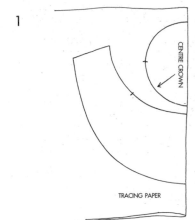

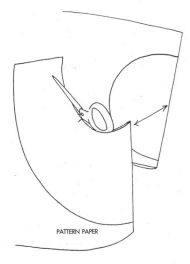

SEAM ALLOWANCES

Collar edge – 1.5 cm (⅝") on basic brim, basic side crown
and the under berets.
1 cm (⅜") on peaks

Centre back seam – 1 cm (⅜") on all patterns.

Outside edge of brim, peak, top crown & top berets –
0.5 cm (¾")

CUTTING THE PATTERN IN FABRIC

MATERIALS AND EQUIPMENT

• Fashion fabric

• Matching sewing thread

• Vilene of medium weight (non-woven interfacing)

• Apparel wadding or wadding 0.5 cm (¼") thick

• Scissors

• Needles

• Pins

• Steam iron and a pressing cloth

• Sewing machine

3

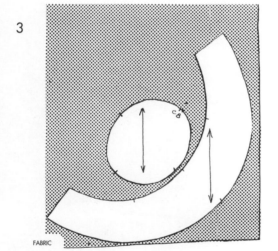

FABRIC

4

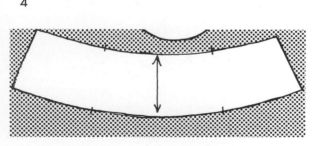

Place the pattern pieces onto the fashion fabric, making
sure the straight grain line on the pattern is in line with
the straight weave of the fabric. (diagrams 3 & 4)

Cut out each pattern piece, **handling each piece very carefully**. The fabric pattern has a bias and some fabrics tend to go out of shape with the slightest movement.

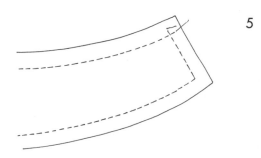

5

Because the fabric pattern is inclined to stretch out of shape with handling, I have found it beneficial to cut a Vilene piece (non-woven medium-weight interfacing) of each pattern, and machine stitch the fabric to this. The Vilene keeps the fabric pattern in shape and it is well worth the effort. (diagrams 5 & 6)

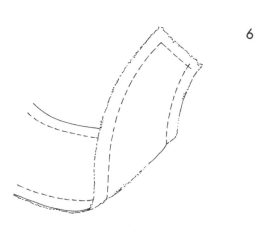

6

The easiest interfacing to use is iron-on fusible Vilene but this does not bond well to all fabrics so it's best to do a test piece.

Use a scrap of the fabric and Vilene – 10 cm (4") is enough. Lay the Vilene down on a flat ironing surface, adhesive side up, then lay the fabric over this, right side up. Carefully ease the fabric to fit the Vilene.

Carefully lay an ironing cloth over and **press** the two together. Test with both steam and dry iron.

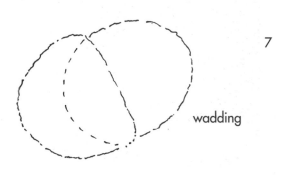

wadding

7

Sometimes the fabric will shrink in at the edges from the Vilene. If this happens, use the Vilene shape as the pattern guide and the Vilene edge as the sewing guide for seam allowances, as the Vilene shape is generally the more stable.

Cut out the necessary pattern pieces in apparel wadding, approximately 0.5 cm ($\frac{1}{4}$") thick.

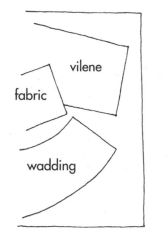

8

vilene

fabric

wadding

If this thickness is not available, split the thicker wadding in half and put the firmer edge to the fabric side of the pattern. (diagram 7)

You should now have one of each pattern piece in fabric, Vilene and wadding. (diagram 8)

9

On each side of the C/B seam of the wadding for the brim and side crown, mark in 1 cm ($\frac{3}{8}$") seam allowance with a dressmakers' fading felt tip marking pen.

Overlap the C/B seams, aligning the stitch lines, and pin into place. (diagram 9)

10

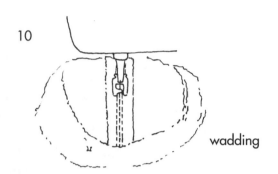

wadding

If you are an experienced machinist, instead of using a marking pen to define the seam stitch line, you will find it quicker to just clip at each end of the seam allowance, on the stitch line, and overlap at these points.

Machine stitch down the C/B stitch line first, then turn and stitch down either side. (diagram 10)

11

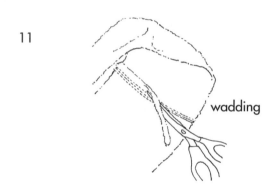

wadding

Carefully clip the excess wadding back from the stitch line on either side.

This avoids bulk on the seam line. (diagram 11)

Sew the C/B seam 1 cm ($\frac{3}{8}$") for the brim and side crown.

12

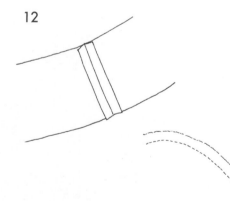

Press the seams open. (diagram 12)

It is a good idea to trim back the Vilene to the stitch line – once again, to avoid bulk at the seams. Lift it away from the fabric seam but if it has really stuck, just leave it. (diagram 13)

13

Carefully align the wadding pieces to the fabric pieces – brim, side crown and the top crown – joining at the notches. Pin to hold in place. (diagram 14)

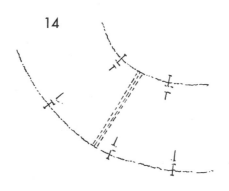

14

Stitch each section together just inside the seam allowance, using a long machine stitch. As you will be unpicking this stitch later, a contrasting thread is useful. (diagram 15)

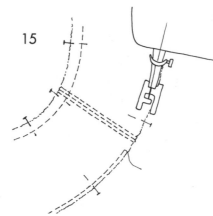

15

THE CROWN

Join the top crown to the side crown, pinning at the notches.

Sew together with a 0.5 cm (¼") seam allowance using a normal length machine stitch.

Match double notches on top crown to the C/B seam. As you sew, ease one to fit the other between notches. (diagram 16)

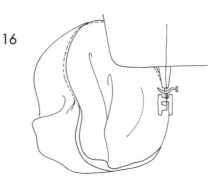

16

Trim back the wadding to the stitch line on the top crown and side crown. (diagram 17)

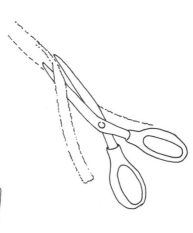

17

Turn the crown through to the right side. (diagram 18)

18

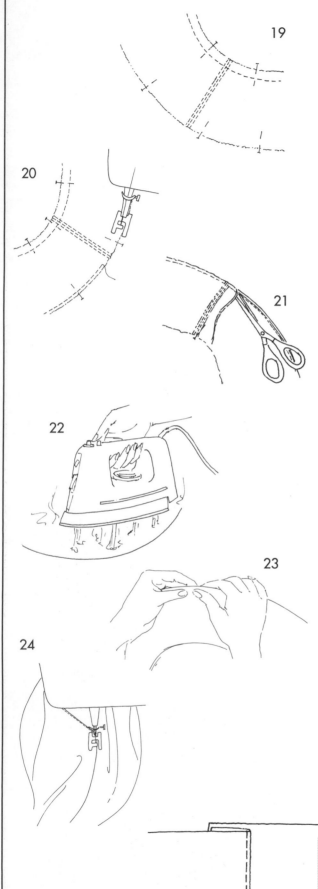

19

20

21

22

23

24

25

THE BRIM

Pin the two fabric brims together, right side to right side, joining at the C/B seam first, then to the C/F notches. Ease one to the other so that they fit comfortably.

Position wadding section over the brim and ease to fit and then pin the three together. (diagram 19)

Sew around the brim edge, using a normal machine stitch length, with a 0.5 cm (¼") seam allowance. Use the edge of the machine foot on the brim edge as a guide when sewing. (diagram 20)

If you are sewing a brim for a child, sew about a 1.5 cm (⅝") seam allowance at the brim edge. This gives a narrower brim and will save you re-cutting a 'graded' pattern.

Carefully trim back excess wadding to the machine stitch line and, if possible, peel back the Vilene and trim it back to the stitch line also. (diagram 21)

Turn brim through to the right side. Then, holding a steam iron above the brim edge let the steam penetrate the fabric but do not press the brim with the iron at this stage. (diagram 22)

Finger press and ease the brim seam to sit as flat as possible. Be patient as, depending on the fabric, it may take a little time but do avoid pressing it with an iron at this stage. (diagram 23)

TURN-UP BRIM

Edge stitch around one side of a brim – the side that won't be seen. This will make the brim edge roll back nicely when you turn it back. The side with the wadding generally looks better to the outside but you decide as it can depend on the type of fabric. (diagram 24)

With the seam edges to one side, stitch close to the seam on the right side. This holds the seam in place. (diagram 25)

Pin the collar edge of the brim in place, aligning notches.

Before stitching the brim to crown, stitch the brim just inside the collar edge seam allowance, using a long machine stitch. This stabilises the brim when sewing the brim to the crown. (diagram 26)

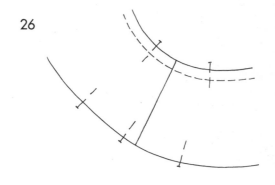

26

STITCHED BRIM

Pin the brim edge in place at C/B seam, C/F and in between these in a couple of places.

Adjust the stitch length on the machine to just a little longer than normal. Stitch the brim by machine, sewing from the C/B and following the shape of the brim in a continuous line of stitching, with a space between each row.

Continuous rows of stitching

Begin with the bulk of the brim to the left, 2 to 3 cm (1 to 1¼") before the C/B, and about 2 mm (¹/₁₆") from the edge of the brim. Continue sewing on the edge of the brim to the beginning. (diagram 27)

Put the machine needle in the last stitch, then sew slowly, moving slightly away from the first row of stitching until the edge of the machine foot is on the edge of the first row of machine stitching. This should happen at about the C/B seam. (diagram 28)

Continue sewing around the brim, with the edge of the machine foot on the previous row of stitching, to the stitching at the collar edge.

Because the brim is not perfectly round, as you get closer to the collar edge it will be necessary to stop at the collar edge seam line, then move to the next section of the brim where the machine foot sits on the previous machine stitch line. (diagram 29)

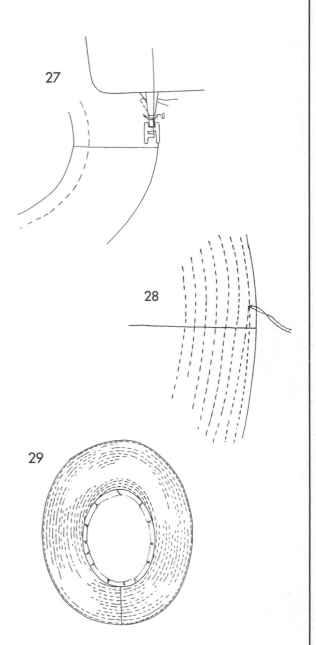

27

28

29

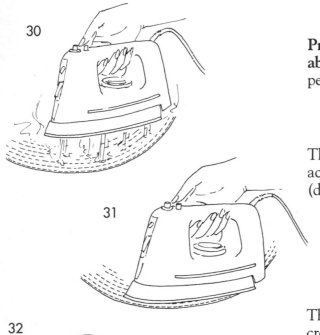

30

Press the brim carefully with a steam iron. Hold the iron **above** the brim by about 2.5 cm (1") and let the steam penetrate the fabric. (diagram 30)

Then press the brim with the iron, in an up and down action. Be careful not to push the brim out of shape. (diagram 31)

31

JOINING BRIM TO CROWN

The following procedure applies to all styles of brims and crowns.

32

Pin the crown to the brim, join the C/B seams first, then C/F and side notches. Ease the crown to fit the brim and pin in between the notches. Be patient and take the time to fit one to the other. (diagram 32)

33

Sew inside the crown using a normal machine stitch length with 1.5 cm (⅝") seam allowance. (diagram 33)

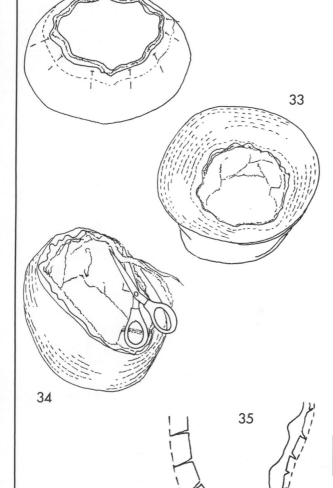

Carefully trim back the wadding on both the brim and the crown to the collar edge seam line to avoid bulk. Where possible, trim back the Vilene also. (diagram 34)

Clip the brim collar edge seam allowance to within 2 mm (¹⁄₁₆") of the stitch line. (diagram 35)

34

35

Do not clip the crown.

CLIP COLLAR SEAM
OF BRIM

Put the hat on an ironing surface with the top crown down and the brim up.

Hold the steam iron over the collar edge seam and let the steam penetrate the fabric. (diagram 36)

Then finger press the collar edge into the inside of the crown.

Put the hat onto the collar, matching the C/B of the hat to the C/B of the collar, and then place the collar on the stand. Let it sit there for awhile to allow the collar edge seams to flatten a little. (diagram 37)

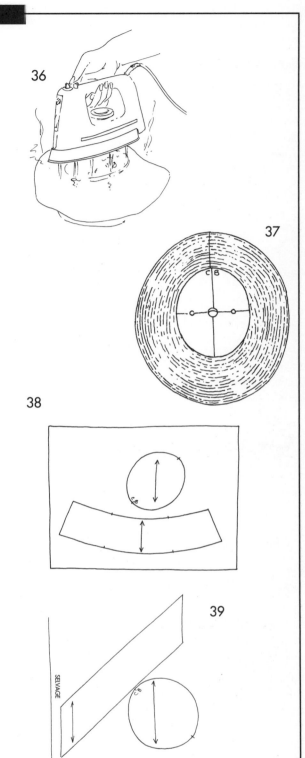

LINING THE CROWN

The purpose in lining the crown is to hide all the seams and to allow the hat to slide smoothly over the head.

There are two lining styles. One is to duplicate the crown pattern. This allows the hat to sit better on the head and to keep its shape. (diagram 38)

The other is to use a bias strip of fabric – the same size as the side crown measurement. This is fitted to a top crown slightly smaller than the collar outline. (diagram 39)

There are also two ways of sewing the lining into the crown.

Cut your lining in a soft fabric – lining taffeta is often a good choice.

FOR EITHER STYLE

Sew C/B seam of side crown. (diagram 40)

Sew bias side crown. (diagram 40a)

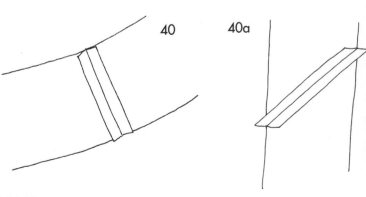

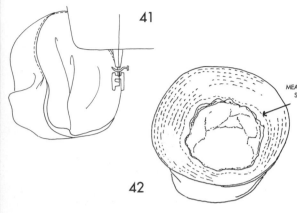

Sew the top crown to the side crown. (diagram 41)

MEASURE COLLAR EDGE
SEAM STITCH LINE

Measure the length of the collar edge seam stitch line on the brim edge of the hat, starting at the C/B seam. (diagram 42)

Method 1

Use nylon petersham ribbon. If your petersham is a cotton/rayon blend, pre-shrink the ribbon before you use it. Lay the ribbon on a flat ironing surface and hold a steam iron over it until it is quite saturated with the steam. Leave it flat to dry.

This method can be done with either style of lining. Cut a length of petersham ribbon – no less than 1.5 cm (⅝") wide – to the measurement of the inside collar edge seam line + 3 cm (1⅛") for overlap at C/B.

Fold ribbon in half and press to determine the C/F on the ribbon. (diagram 43)

Join the ribbon with a 1.5 cm (⅝") seam allowance. Press the seam to one side. (diagrams 44 & 45)

Lay the petersham ribbon on the right side of the lining, 1.5 cm (⅝") above the collar edge. Pin to mark C/F. Pin ribbon into place, easing the lining to fit the ribbon. Machine stitch the ribbon to the lining, stitching 2 mm (1/16") in from the ribbon edge. (diagram 46)

Press the lining up from the ribbon edge. (diagram 47)

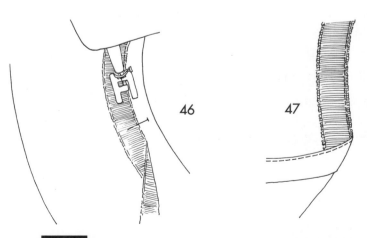

Pin the ribbon edge of lining into the crown, just a little (very little) below the collar edge stitch line, with C/B seams aligned, and C/F mark on ribbon and crown aligned. Pin securely all the way around the inside crown, making sure that the outside crown is flat and smooth and not caught up.

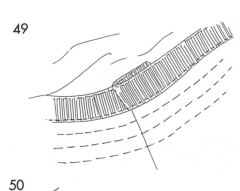

48

Carefully machine the two together, stitching on the very edge of the ribbon, checking often to make sure the underside of the crown is smooth and not caught up. Be patient and sew slowly. (diagrams 48 & 49)

49

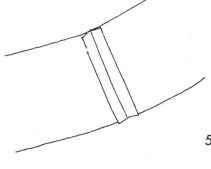

Method 2
Hand sew the lining into the crown. Then hand or machine stitch the petersham ribbon on the collar edge stitch line. If you hand stitch the lining, sew two rows of machine stitching when sewing the crown to the brim for more stability. (diagram 49)

50

Sew C/B seam of side crown. (diagram 50)

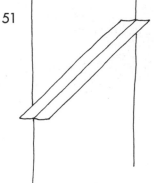

51

Sew bias side crown. (diagram 51)

Sew the top crown to the side crown. (diagram 52)

52

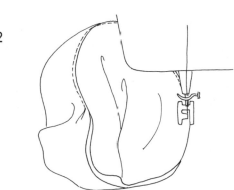

53

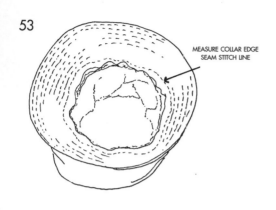

MEASURE COLLAR EDGE
SEAM STITCH LINE

Measure the length of the collar edge seam stitch line on the brim edge of the hat, starting at the C/B seam. (diagram 53)

Cut a length of petersham ribbon – no less than 1.5 cm (⅝") wide – to the measurement of the inside collar edge seam + 3 cm (1¼") for the overlap at C/B.

54

Fold ribbon in half and press to determine the C/F on the ribbon. (diagram 54)

55

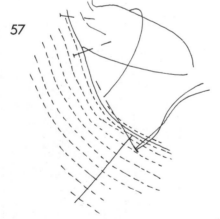

Join the ribbon with a 1.5 cm (⅝") seam allowance. Press seam to one side. (diagrams 55 & 56)

56

Pin the lining into the crown, with the C/F and C/B notches aligned.

57

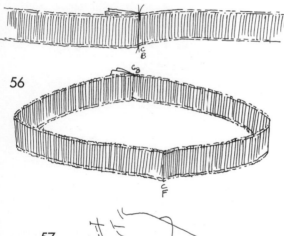

Hand stitch the lining into the crown, just above the collar edge seam stitching. (diagram 57)

Pin the petersham ribbon just a little (very little) below the collar edge seam stitching, aligning C/F marks and C/B seams. Hand or machine stitch the ribbon into place. (diagram 58)

58

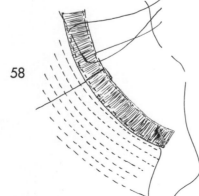

Place the completed hat on an ironing surface with the top crown down and brim up.

Hold the steam iron over the petersham ribbon on the collar edge and let the steam penetrate the fabric. (diagram 59)

Then finger press the ribbon into the inside of the crown.

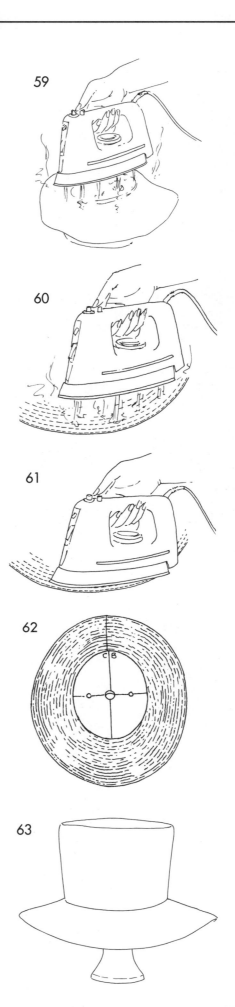

59

60

61

62

63

Press the brim carefully with a steam iron. Hold the iron about 2.5 cm (1") **above** the brim and let the steam penetrate the fabric. (diagram 60)

Then press the brim with the iron, in an up and down action. Be careful not to push the brim out of shape. (diagram 61)

Put the collar into the hat on the petersham ribbon collar edge, matching C/B seam of the hat to the C/B of the collar. (diagram 62)

Place hat on stand and ease the brim into shape gently with fingers, if and where necessary. (diagram 63)

You now have the basic brim and the basic crown sewn together. You'll find that different fabrics and trims make this design very versatile.

BERET CONSTRUCTION

The construction of a beret depends on the fabric chosen, and the way in which the beret is to sit on the head.

A beret can be worn pulled down to either side, to the back or forward to the front. It can also have a peak attached.

A beret looks rather smart standing straight up.

When the beret has a 'soft' look, interface with a thin wadding, fusible looks the best, especially on velvet.

Sew the under beret side seam, press open. (diagram 64)

Trim back interfacing to stitch line if possible. Pin top beret and under beret together, aligning notches. Machine stitch the two together. (diagram 65)

PIPING TRIM

If you are sewing a piping trim, use a different colour thread in the bobbin and increase the machine stitch length when sewing the piping in place. Use the machine 'zipper foot' to sew the piping in place. (diagram 66)

In my experience it is easier to sew the piping to the **under beret**.

Pin the top beret in place, aligning notches, and stitch the two together, using the different colour thread as a guide to the edge of where the piping is. (diagram 67)

Trim back any excess to the stitch line, as always, to avoid bulk.

If you are using handmade felt, be careful when using fusible interfacing. Use a cloth and a dry iron. The steam can sometimes shrink the felt. Always test the fabric and the interfacing on scrap fabric before you start bonding the pattern pieces.

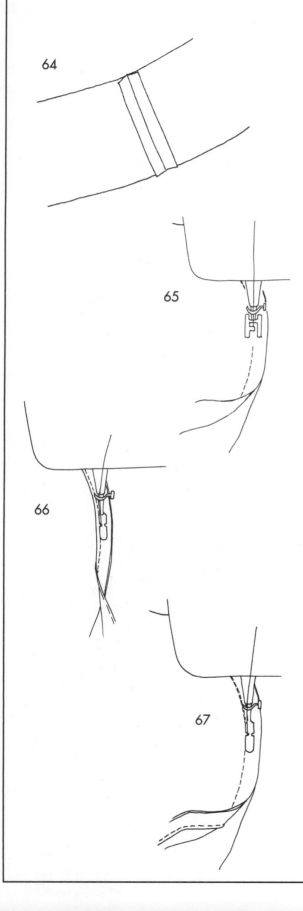

64

65

66

67

HEADBAND/BANDEAU

Interface the headband/bandeau, sew the seam and press the seam flat. Fold and press the headband/bandeau in half. Stitch along the seam edge, just inside the seam allowance to hold in place.

For effect, the headband can be stitched.

Pin the headband to the collar edge of the under beret aligning notches. Sew the two together. (diagram 68)

68

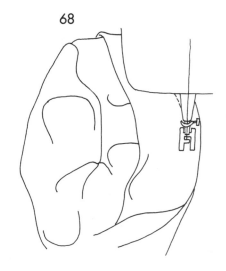

LINING

Cut the top and under beret pattern pieces in a lining fabric, sew the seam of the under beret, press the seam open.

Sew the top beret to the under beret. At the front edge of the top beret seam, unpick the stitching to make an opening about 10 cm to 12 cm (4" to 4¾") long. (diagram 69)

69

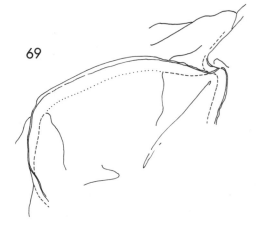

Attaching lining

Fold the headband/bandeau up/back so that it is resting on the right side of the under beret, place the lining over the beret, right side of the lining to the right side of the beret. Pin in place, matching the notches at the collar edge of the lining and the beret. The headband is encased between the two. The seams raw edges of the lining are on the outside facing you.

Sew the two, with the headband, together on the inside edge of the beret, following the headband stitch line. (diagram 70)

70

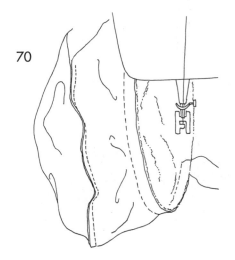

71

Diagram 71 illustrates a peak attached to a headband.

72

When they are sewn together, put your hand carefully through the unpicked section of the lining and gently pull the beret through. Pull a little at a time. (diagram 72)

73

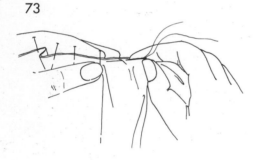

Close the opening in the lining with a slip stitch. Press the lining into the inside of the beret. (diagram 73)

74

The finished beret. (diagram 74)

PLATE 9

PLATE 10

PLATE 11

PLATE 12

CHAPTER 9

CONSTRUCTING PIECE CROWNS, PEAKS AND BERETS

THE PIECE CROWN

Piece crowns can be attached to brims or peaks and can have fabric or knitted roll-up bands attached.

If your piece crown isn't going to be lined – e.g. with a peak sports cap – it's a good idea to overlock each raw side seam. Use the differential feed so as not to stretch the fabric pattern piece.

Fuse wadding and/or Vilene to fabric pattern pieces. (diagram 1)

Stitch crown pieces together from collar edge to top notch. (diagram 2)

Trim wadding and/or Vilene to stitch line. (diagram 3)

With some fabric it is necessary to clip into the seam allowance to within 2 to 3 mm ($^1/_{16}$") of the stitch line to enable the seams to sit flat when they are pressed open.

Press the seams open with your fingers.

Then place a thick towel over your hand and rest the crown over it. Hold a steam iron over the seam, then when the seams are well steamed, use the point of the iron to flatten the seams open. (diagram 4)

Put collar into the crown and secure with drawing pins. Decide on and mark C/B, C/F and side notches.

Then stand back and look at the style. (diagram 5)

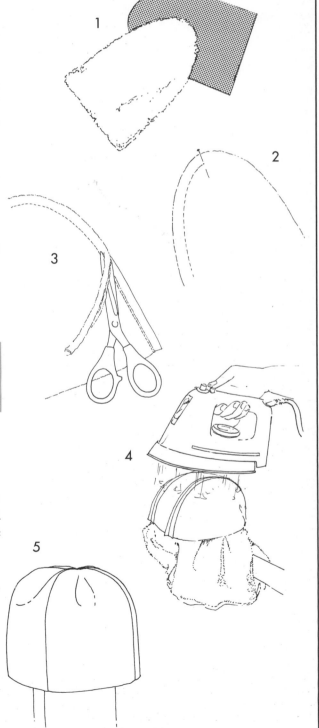

6

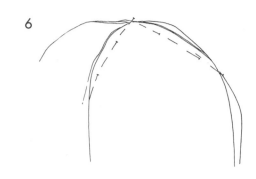

Pin any alterations in place. (diagram 6)

Transfer these alterations to the pattern piece and then place the pattern piece onto folded pattern paper. Trace new pattern lines. Remove pattern and add seam allowances. Cut new pattern piece. Mark straight grain line and notches. (diagram 7)

Repeat the construction method for the remaining pieces.

Piece crowns can be attached to brims or peaks.

7

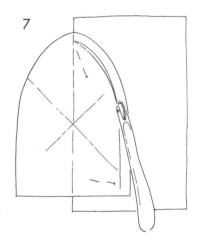

They can have fabric or knitted roll-up bands attached.

PEAK FOR CROWNS

Modify the peak for the beret to suit your crown.

Lay pattern piece on folded paper – C/F in line with folded edge. (diagram 8)

8

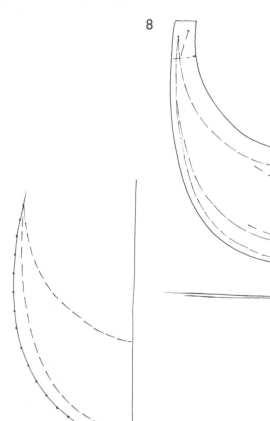

Trace collar edge seam line and brim edge line to the depth required. Broken line is the original design line.

Mark C/F and side notches.

Remove pattern. (diagram 9)

Add seam allowances:
• 1 cm (³⁄₈") collar edge
• 0.5 cm (¹⁄₄") brim edge.

9

CONSTRUCTION OF PEAK

Cut:

- 2 fabric
- 2 Vilene (non-woven interfacing)
- 1 wadding.

Fuse fabric to Vilene.

Place the two fabric pieces together, right sides facing.

Place wadding pattern piece to one Vilene side.

Pin all three together, aligning notches.

Stitch around the brim edge, 0.5 cm (¼") seam allowance.

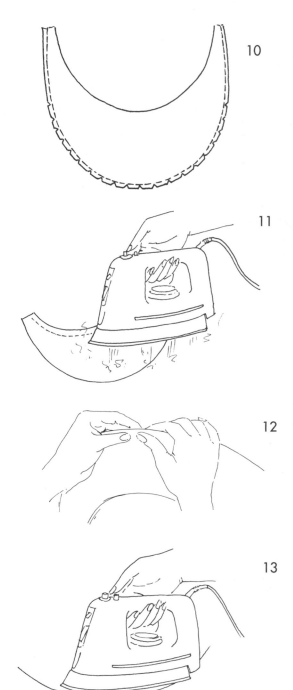

10

When stitching a curved edge, use a smaller than normal machine stitch length. The small stitch gives a rounded seam edge to the curve.

Trim wadding to stitch line and Vilene, if possible, to avoid bulk. Clip into stitch line in the shape of a 'V' about every 1.5 cm (⅝") around the curved edge. (diagram 10)

Turn peak to right side.

11

Hold steam iron over peak and let steam penetrate the fabric. (diagram 11)

12

Finger press the peak edge. (diagram 12)

When the seam edge is smoothed and each side in line at the peak/brim edge, **press** the peak flat with the steam iron. (diagram 13)

13

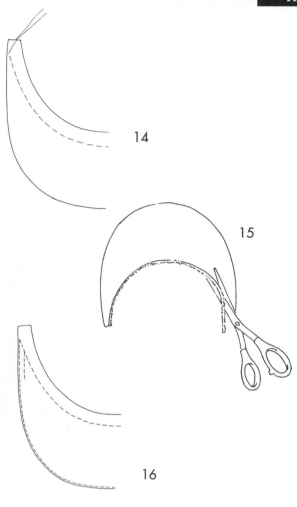

Stitch along collar edge to just within the collar edge seam allowance. (diagram 14)

There may be excess wadding showing around the collar edge. Trim this back to be in line with the fabric collar edge. (diagram 15)

Stitch from the collar edge stitch line, around the peak edge to the collar edge stitch line on the other side.

It is tidier if you turn, stitch along the collar edge stitch line to the width of the stitching required, turn and sew in line with the stitch line to the other side of the peak. (diagram 16)

Continue in this way until the peak is completely stitched all the way around.

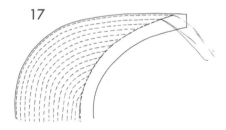

Pull the threads through, **but do not cut these off**. These are useful when you are sewing the peak to the crown. (diagram 17)

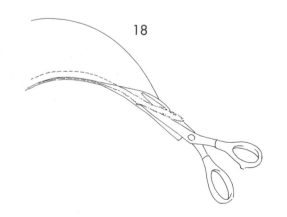

Trim back the wadding to the stitch line in between the fabric collar edge, to avoid bulk. (diagram 18)

Attach peak to crown as you would a brim, C/F notches first, then to the side notch. Ease one to fit the other.

A 1 cm (⅝") seam allowance on the collar edge of the peak makes it easier to sew to the crown. (diagram 19)

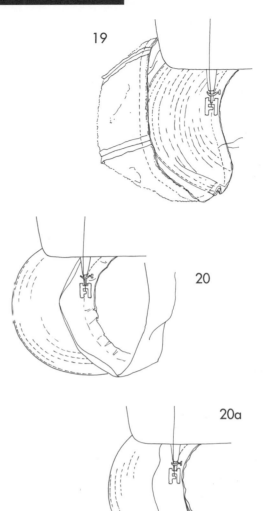

19

ATTACHING PEAK TO HEADBAND/BANDEAU

Cut 2 headbands/bandeaux in fabric – interface each headband – sew the seam of each headband then press seams open.

Position the finished peak to one headband/bandeau and machine stitch in place with a long stitch length, aligning notches. (diagram 20)

20

Place the second headband/bandeau over the first, right side to right side, encasing the peak between, aligning notches and seams. Stitch the two together. (diagram 20a)

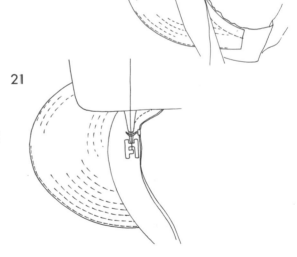

20a

Turn the headband through to the right side and press.

Edge stitch if necessary

21

Secure the two headbands together machine stitching along the raw edge. (diagram 21)

Attach the headband/bandeau to the crown as you would a brim – C/F notches first, then back, then side notches. Ease one to fit the other. (diagram 22)

A 1 cm (⅜") seam allowance on the collar edge of the headband/bandeau makes it easier to sew to the crown.

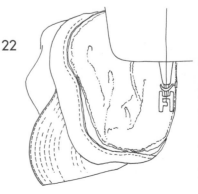

22

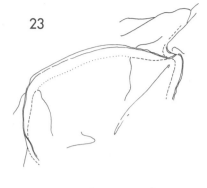

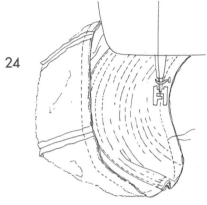

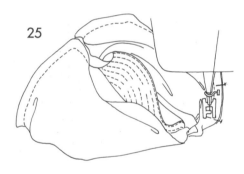

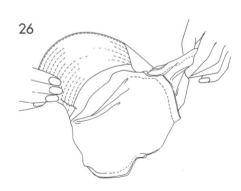

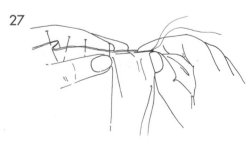

LINING A 'PIECE' CROWN

If you are lining your piece crown, cut additional pattern pieces in a lightweight fabric – lining taffeta is a good choice.

Sew them together, following the instructions for the piece crown.

Press seams open and unpick one seam to within 1.5 cm ($\frac{5}{8}$") at top crown and collar edge. (diagram 23)

Sew the peak to the crown, aligning C/F and side notches. (diagram 24)

Lay the lining crown over the fabric crown, right side to right side, joining at the seams. Tuck the peak in between.

Pin around the collar edge. Aligning and pinning the centre top of the crown can be useful.

Stitch the two together around the collar edge with 1 cm ($\frac{3}{8}$") seam allowance, starting at the C/B. (diagram 25)

Put your hand through the opening in the lining seam, and pull the fabric crown through. (diagram 26)

Hold a steam iron over collar edge seam, then finger press flat. Machine stitch around the collar edge to keep flat.

Close the opening in the lining with hand stitching, or machine stitch seam edge. (diagram 27)

UNLINED 'PIECE' CROWN

If your crown is unlined, you can finish with petersham ribbon or a piece of the same fabric, or you can add a seam allowance that will allow a turned-up hem.

THE THREE-PIECE ROUND CROWN

The method for constructing the three-piece round crown is basically the same as for piece crowns – it's just that the pattern pieces are a different shape.

Cut your pattern pieces with the straight grain in the direction that suits the design.

Bond or press the Vilene to the fashion fabric.

If you are using wadding, pin it to the fabric pattern piece. Machine them together using a long machine stitch just inside the seam allowance. This helps when sewing the pieces together.

If you are stitching your crown pieces, now is the time to do it. Only stitch to the seam allowance stitch line. This allows trimming back of the wadding to the stitch line to avoid bulk.

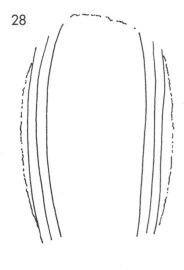

28

THE STITCHED CROWN

All crown styles can be stitched. They can be stitched in line with the shape of the pattern, in a diagonal, in a square, or whatever. Contrasting coloured thread can be very attractive. You do your stitching on the fabric side.

Pin one side crown to one side of the top crown, carefully aligning the notches.

Sew together, using a slightly shorter machine stitch than normal. This gives the finished seam a smoother edge.

Sew the other side crown to the other side of the top crown. (diagram 28)

29

Trim back excess wadding. (diagram 29)

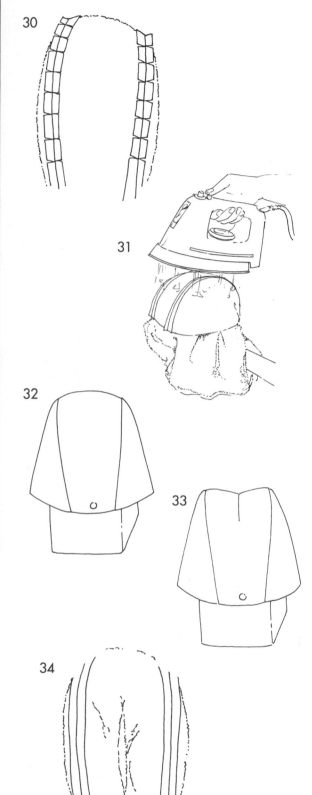

If your fabric pieces are cut with the straight grain going from C/F to C/B on the top crown, and from the collar edge to the top on the side crown, clip into the seam allowance to within 2 to 3 mm ($\frac{1}{16}$") of the stitch line.

When the fabric pattern is cut on the bias, you generally do not have to clip.

The reason for clipping is so that the seams will press open and lay flat without any puckering. (diagram 30)

Press the seams open with your fingers. Place a thick towel over your hand and rest the crown over it. Hold a steam iron over the seams and when the seams are well steamed, use the point of the iron to flatten the seams open. (diagram 31)

Turn the crown through to the right side, place on collar and secure with drawing pins at C/F, C/B and sides.

Have a look at the shape. (diagram 32)

If you want a dip in the centre of the top crown, (diagram 33) wait for the steam to dry out.

When the steam has dried, turn the crown inside out and stitch a dart in the middle and down the centre of the top crown. (diagram 34).

Fit the crown to a peak or a brim of your choice. (diagrams 35 & 36)

CHAPTER 10

GRADING HAT SIZES

Grading is a method whereby the hat pattern pieces can be increased or decreased in size. We will increase one size and decrease one size of our basic brim, side crown and top crown. Once you have graded one size, the process will become clear.

The basic patterns are symmetrical, so we only need to make our grading to one side of our pattern piece.

When you are going to grade a pattern, it is easier if you transfer half the pattern to lightweight card.

Always make the front edge lines, base line etc – all the lines used as base reference points – more defined. I find it useful to use the same coloured pencil on my grade lines as I intend to use to outline the pattern piece I am grading. I continue the colour theme through all the pattern pieces for the one hat design.

THE BRIM

MATERIALS AND EQUIPMENT

- 1 piece of paper to grade the pattern on, 25.5 cm (10") x 43 cm (17")

- 1 dressmakers' square rule

- 2 coloured pencils

- Sticky tape (the type you can write on is best)

- Weights (old plumbing bits and pieces are useful, such as brass taps, elbow joints, etc., or an old clothes iron, or tins of food)

1

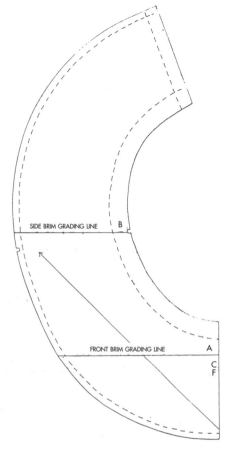

SIDE BRIM GRADING LINE   B

FRONT BRIM GRADING LINE   A
C
F

GRADING LINES

On your pattern at C/F, measure up 7 cm (2¾"). Rule a line square across the brim from C/F.

> It must be square.

This is the front brim grading line (A).

Measure up from this line to the side notch on the collar edge, and the same distance to the brim edge opposite the side notch. Rule a line connecting these points. This is the side brim grading line (B). (diagram 1)

2

FRONT EDGE LINE

Grade paper basic brim

On the grade paper, draw a straight line along the 43 cm (17") length. This is the front edge line. (diagram 2)

Lay the pattern piece onto the grade paper with C/F in line with the front edge line, and hold in place with a weight or small piece of sticky tape.

We need to extend the grading lines on the pattern onto the grade paper.

3

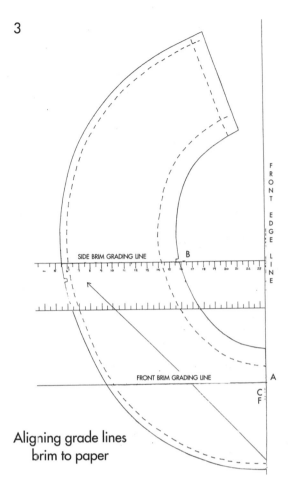

Aligning grade lines
brim to paper

Carefully place a ruler across the pattern on the front brim line and extend the line across onto the grade paper either side of the pattern piece. Do the same on the side brim line and then remove pattern. (diagram 3)

4

Now connect the front brim and side lines on the grade paper. The front brim line (A) and side brim lines (B) now intersect across the front edge line. (diagram 4)

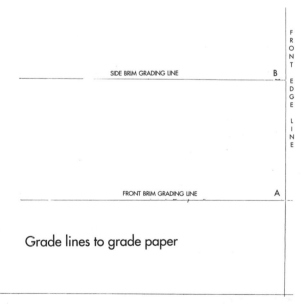

Grade lines to grade paper

5

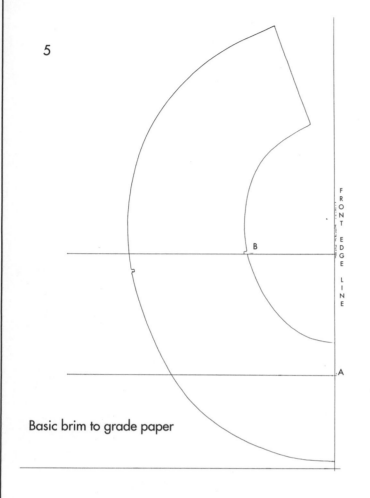

Basic brim to grade paper

Replace pattern, aligning the grade lines. Draw outline of pattern. (diagram 5)

THE FRONT EDGE LINE

The measurement to the right of this line decreases the size of the pattern.

The measurement to the left of this line increases the size of the pattern.

We are going to increase our pattern piece size by 2 cm (¾") overall. We increase 1 cm (⅜") on the side of the pattern we are grading. When we open the pattern out, this increase will also apply to the other side of the pattern.

Then we are going to decrease our pattern by 2 cm (¾") overall.

Start on the front brim line (A). To the **right** of the front edge line measure 0.5 cm (¼").

To the **left** of the front edge line measure 0.5 cm (¼"), 1 cm (⅜") and 1.5 cm (⅝").

Mark these same measurements on the side brim line (B). **Carefully** rule a line connecting each of the measurements in line with the front edge line. These measurements are for increasing or decreasing the front of the brim. Diagram 6 shows detail of front edge lines (A) and side brim lines (B).

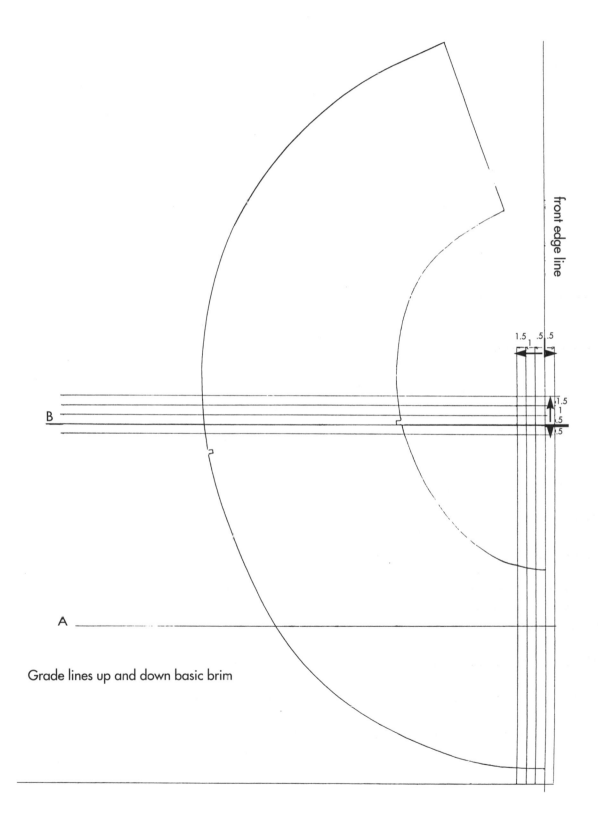

front edge line

1.5 .5 .5
1

1.5
1
.5
.5

B

A

Grade lines up and down basic brim

THE SIDE BRIM LINE

The measurements below this line decrease the size of the pattern. The measurements above this line increase the size of the pattern.

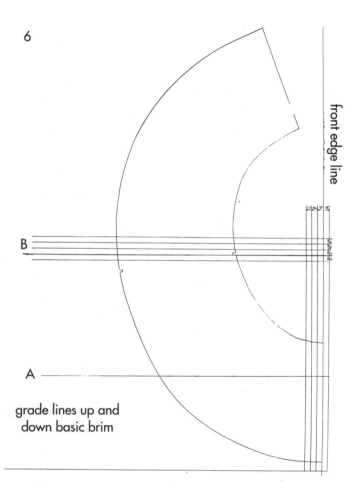

6

front edge line

B

A

grade lines up and
down basic brim

On the side brim line, where it connects with the front edge line, measure below the side brim line (B) 0.5 cm (¼"). Then measure above the side brim line (B) 0.5 cm (¼"), 1 cm (⅜") and 1.5 cm (⅝").

Move across the side brim line approximately 21 cm (8¼") and mark the same measurements **above** and **below** the side brim line.

Carefully rule a line connecting each of the measurements in line with the side brim line. These measurements are for **increasing** or **decreasing** the back of the brim. (diagram 6)

In our examples we will grade up one size then down one size.

Lay the pattern on the grade paper with C/F to the front edge line.

Make sure the front brim line and the side brim line on the pattern are in line with those on the grade paper.

It is very important that these lines are perfectly in line.

INCREASING PATTERN SIZE

Move the pattern piece to the left of the front edge line 0.5 cm (¼").

Make sure the front brim line (A) and side brim line (B) on the pattern and grade paper are perfectly in line.

From the C/F, with the first coloured pencil, outline pattern at collar edge to the side notch.

Do not outline the C/F line edge – the line on the grade paper becomes the C/F line.

Then outline from C/F at the brim edge to brim edge side notch. (diagram 7)

Move the pattern up to the 0.5 cm (¼") line above the side brim line (B).

Make sure the side brim line is perfectly in line with the 0.5 cm (¼") line and the front edge line is perfectly in line with the 0.5 cm (¼") line.

Outline the remainder of the pattern from the side notch at the collar edge, around the centre back to the side notch on the brim edge. (diagram 8)

Remove the pattern and redraw this outline, adjusting if and where necessary.

Measure midway between the notches and mark. These become the new notch marks for the new pattern size.

7

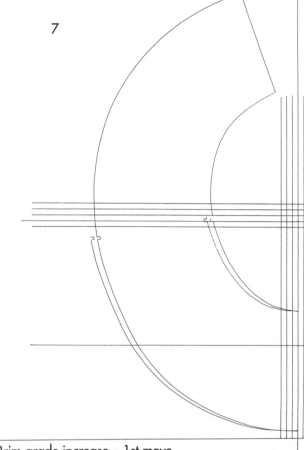

Brim grade increase – 1st move

8

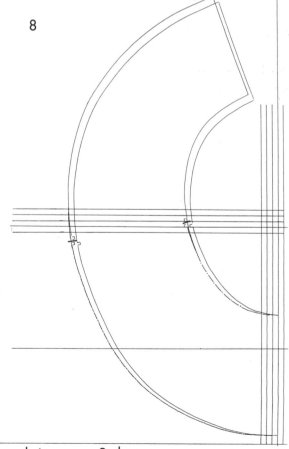

Brim grade increase – 2nd move

9

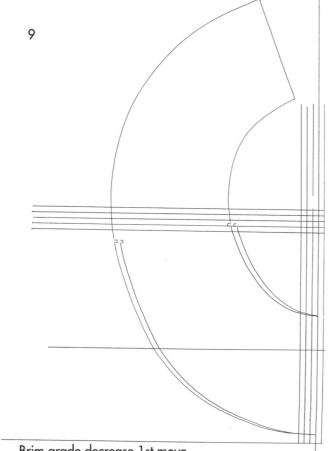

Brim grade decrease 1st move

DECREASING PATTERN SIZE

Move the pattern piece to the right of the front edge line 0.5 cm (¼"). Make sure the front brim line (A) and side brim line (B) on the pattern and grade paper are perfectly in line.

From the front edge line, with the second coloured pencil, outline pattern at the collar edge to the side notch. Do not outline the C/F line edge – the line on the grade paper becomes the C/F line.

Then outline from front edge line at the brim edge to brim edge side notch. (diagram 9)

10

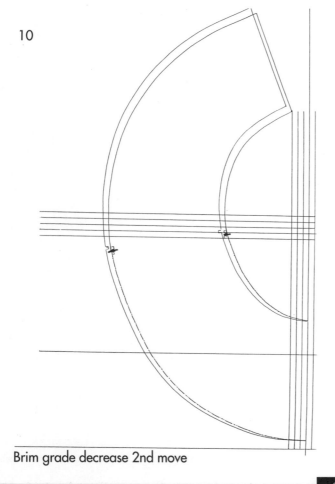

Brim grade decrease 2nd move

Move the pattern down to the 0.5 cm (¼") line below the side brim line (B).

Make sure the side brim line (B) is perfectly in line with the 0.5 cm (1/4") line and the front edge line is perfectly in line with the 0.5 cm (1/4") to the right of the front edge line.

Outline the remainder of the pattern from the side notch on the collar edge, around the centre back to the side notch at the brim edge. (diagram 10)

Remove pattern.

Redraw this outline, adjusting if and where necessary.

Measure midway between the notches and mark. These become the new notch marks for the new pattern size.

Diagram 11 below illustrates one grade size down and three grade sizes up.

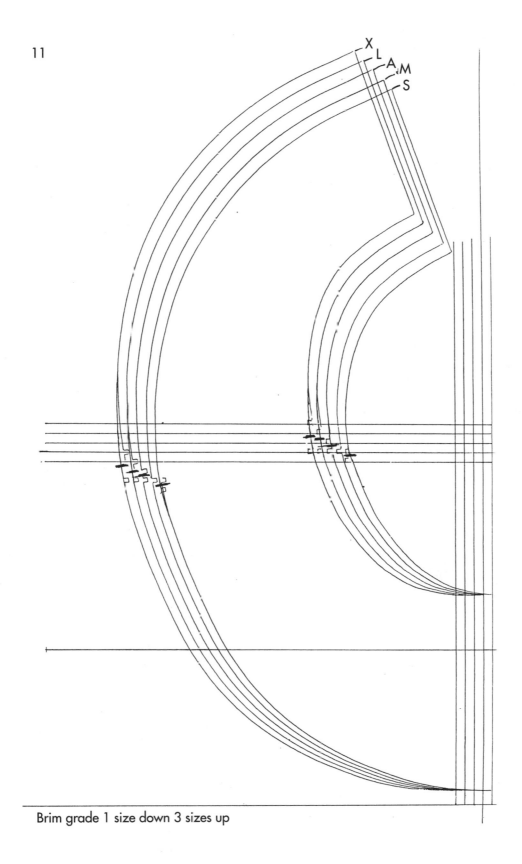

Brim grade 1 size down 3 sizes up

THE SIDE CROWN

The grading method for the side crown is the same as for the brim.

We increase or decrease the pattern size at the front and the back of the side crown. Only one grading line is needed.

GRADING LINES

On your pattern at C/F, measure up 5 cm (2") from the collar edge and rule a line square across the pattern piece from C/F across to C/B on side crown. It must be square. This is the side crown grading line. (diagram 12)

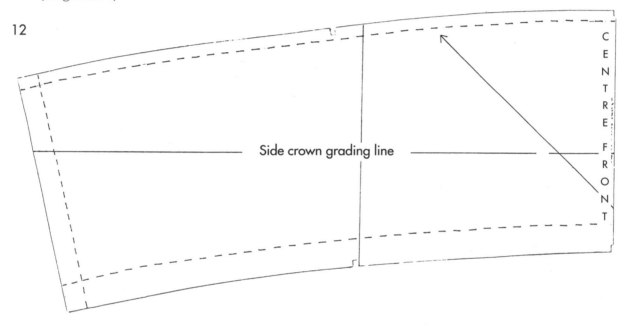

12

Side crown grading line

C
E
N
T
R
E
F
R
O
N
T

On the grade paper, measure in 2 cm (¾") and draw a straight line along the 43 cm (17") length. This is the front edge line. (diagram 13)

13

Front edge line

Grade paper basic side crown

Lay the pattern piece onto the grade paper with C/F in line with the front edge line, and hold in place with a weight or small piece of sticky tape.

We need to extend the grading lines on the pattern onto the grade paper.

Carefully lay a ruler across the pattern on the side crown grading line and extend the line across onto the grade paper either side of the pattern piece. (diagram 14)

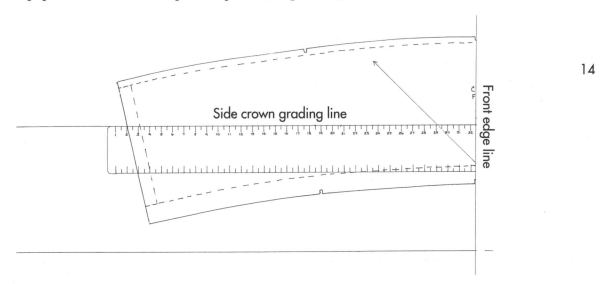

14

Draw around the outline of the pattern piece and then remove pattern.

Now connect the side crown line on the grade paper.

The side crown grading line now intersects across the front edge line. (diagram 15)

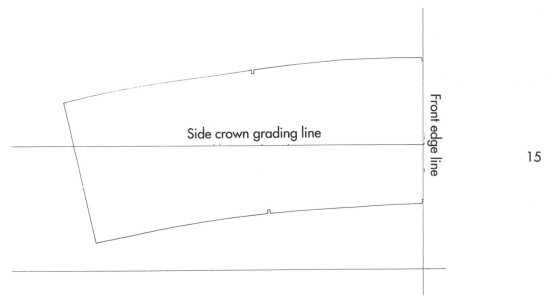

15

We are going to increase and decrease the size of our pattern piece by 2 cm (¾") overall. We increase 1 cm (⅜") on the side of the pattern we are grading.

When we open the pattern out, this increase or decrease will also apply to the other side of the pattern.

THE FRONT EDGE LINE

The measurement to the **right** of the front edge line decreases the size of the pattern. The measurement to the **left** of this line increases the size of the pattern.

On the side crown line from the front edge line, measure to the **right** 0.5 cm and 1 cm (¼" and ⅜"), then to the **left** 0.5 cm, 1 cm, 1.5 cm, 2 cm, 2.5 cm and 3 cm (¼", ⅜", ⅝", ¾", 1" and 1⅛")

Move up the front edge line about 10 cm (4") and repeat and mark these measurements. Carefully rule lines connecting these marks. It is helpful to mark the 0.5 cm, 1.5 cm and 2.5 cm (¼", ⅝" and 1") lighter than the others. (diagram 16)

16

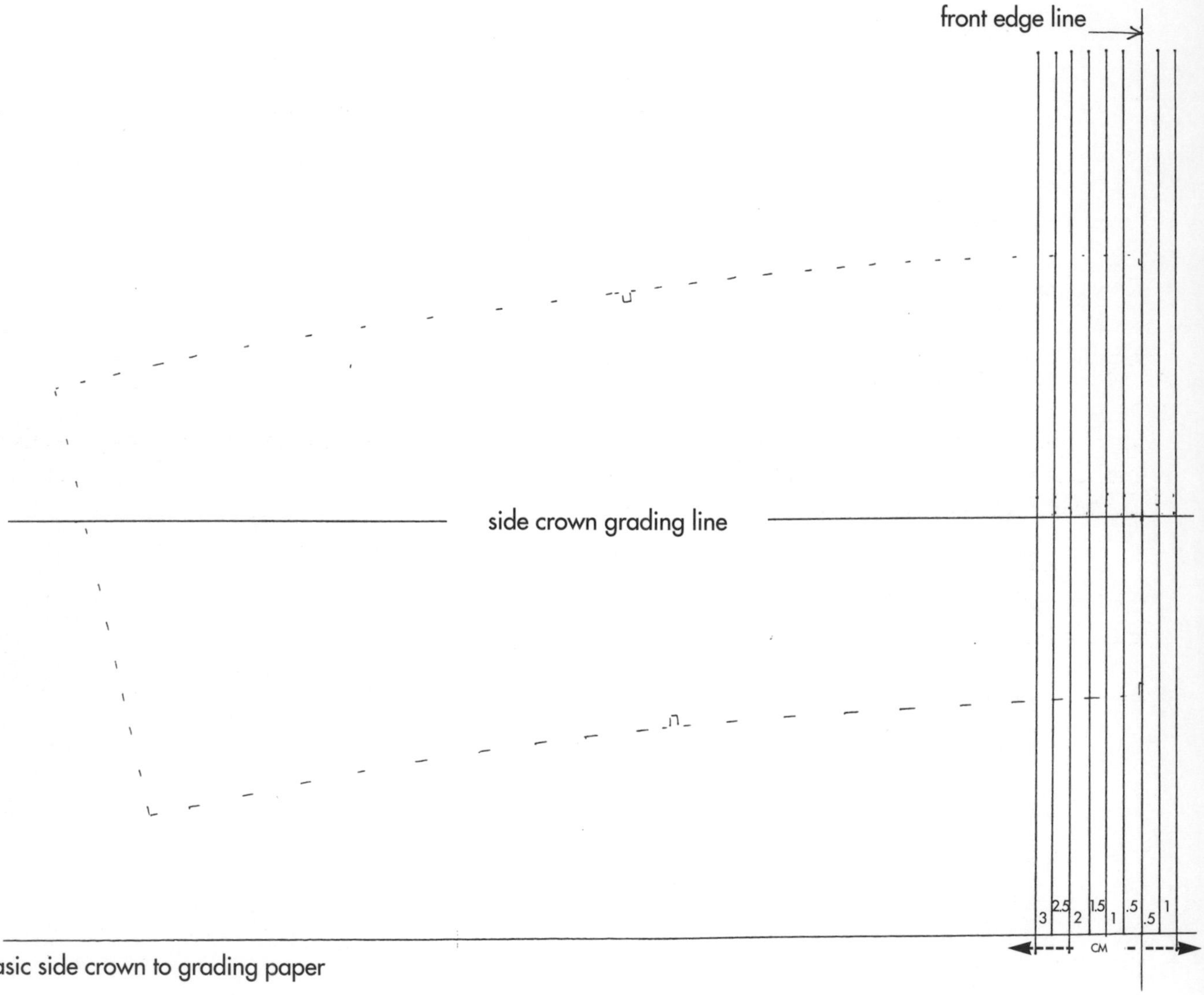

front edge line

side crown grading line

3 2.5 2 1.5 1 .5 .5 1

CM

Basic side crown to grading paper

Lay the pattern on the grade paper with C/F to the front edge line, making sure the crown lines on the pattern and the grade paper are in line.

It is very important that these are perfectly in line with each other. (diagram 17)

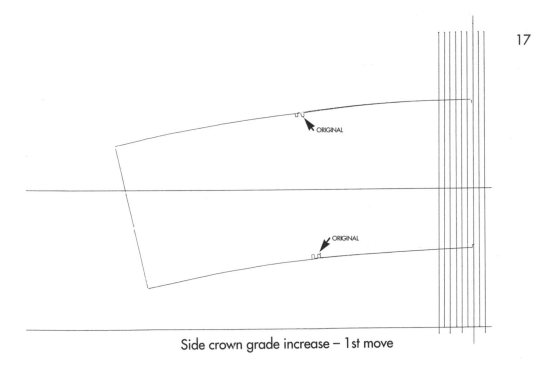

Side crown grade increase – 1st move

INCREASING PATTERN SIZE

Use the same pencil colour as you used for the first brim grading.

Move the pattern to the left 0.5 cm (¼") from the front edge line, keeping side crown lines perfectly in line. Outline the pattern on the collar edge from the C/F to the side notch then to the top edge, from C/F to the top side notch. (diagram 18)

Then move the pattern to the left to the 1 cm (⅜") line and continue to outline pattern on the collar edge from the side notch to C/B, up to top edge to top side notch.

Remove pattern.

Redraw this outline, adjusting if and where necessary. Measure midway between the notches and mark. These become the new notch marks for the new pattern size.

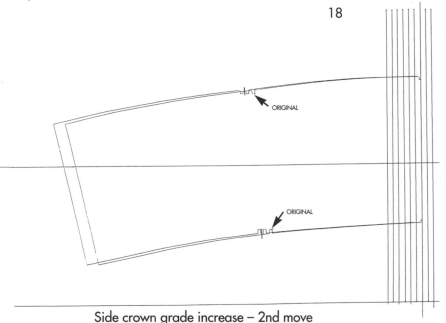

Side crown grade increase – 2nd move

DECREASING PATTERN SIZE

Use the second pencil colour you used for the first brim grading.

Move pattern to the right 1 cm (⅜") from the front edge line, keeping side crown lines perfectly in line. Outline the complete pattern piece, with notches. (diagram 19)

Then move the pattern to the left of the 0.5 cm (¼") line and only mark notches on collar edge and top edge.

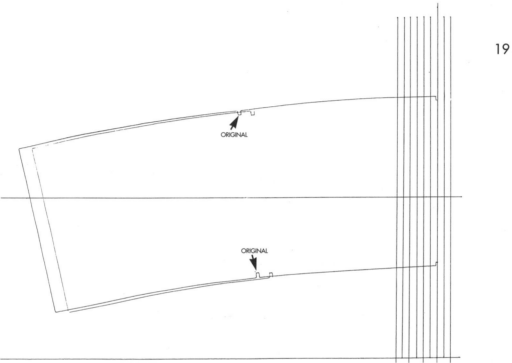

Side crown decrease – 1st move

Remove pattern and redraw this outline, adjusting if and where necessary. Measure midway between the notches and mark. These become the new notch marks for the new pattern size. (diagram 20)

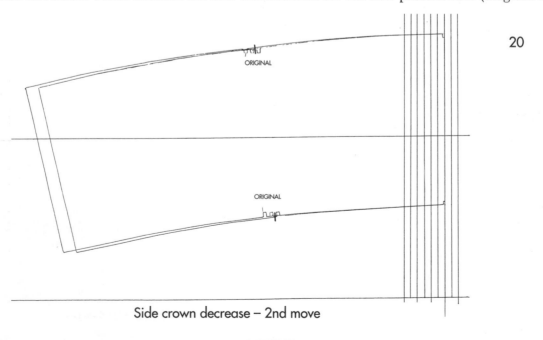

Side crown decrease – 2nd move

Diagram 21 illustrates one grade down and three grades up.

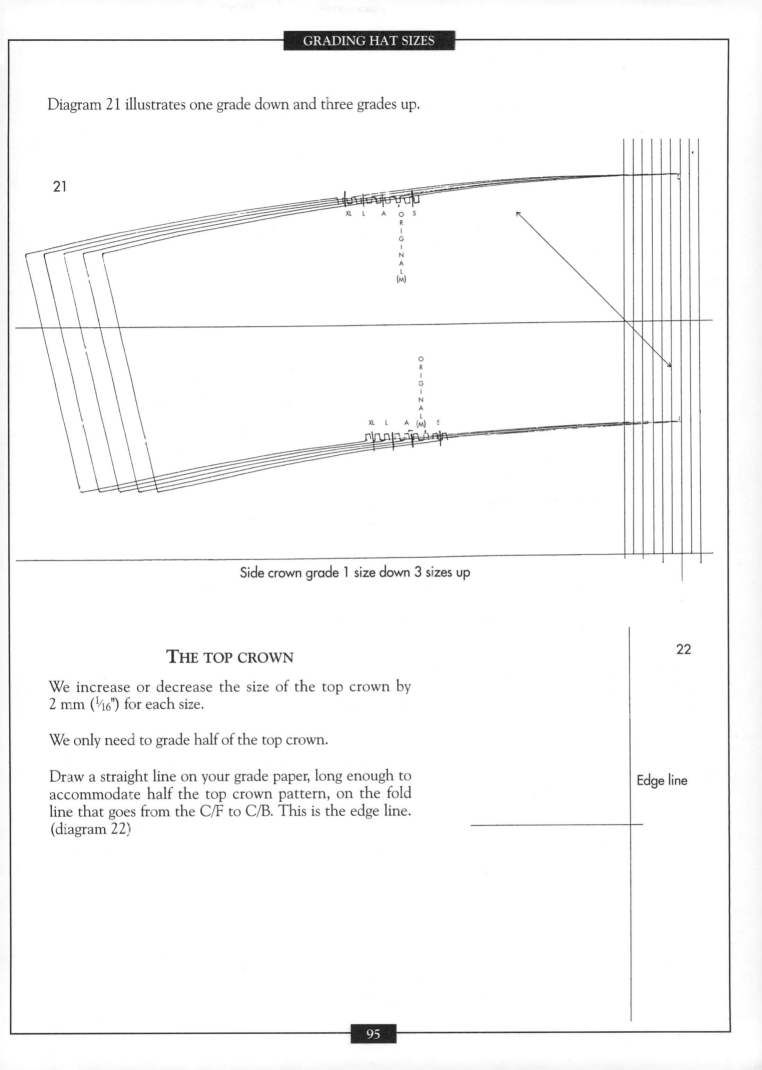

Side crown grade 1 size down 3 sizes up

THE TOP CROWN

We increase or decrease the size of the top crown by 2 mm ($\frac{1}{16}$") for each size.

We only need to grade half of the top crown.

Draw a straight line on your grade paper, long enough to accommodate half the top crown pattern, on the fold line that goes from the C/F to C/B. This is the edge line. (diagram 22)

23

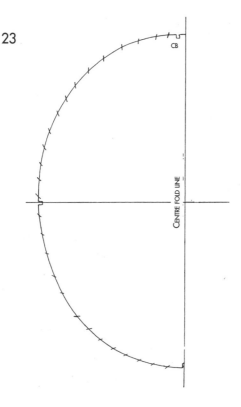

Top crown grade – collar

24

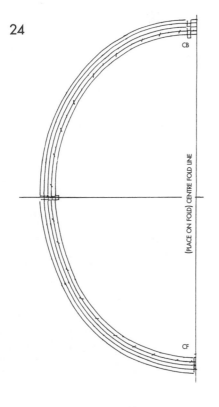

Place half the pattern piece in a line along the edge line. Draw around the outline of the top crown. (diagram 23)

INCREASING PATTERN SIZE

Measure out 2 mm ($\frac{1}{16}$") around the outside of the top crown outline. (diagram 24)

DECREASING PATTERN SIZE

Measure right 2 mm ($\frac{1}{16}$") right around the inside of the top crown outline. (diagram 24)

Compare the measurement of the stitch line on the graded top crown with the stitch line on the top edge of the side crown. Make any adjustments that may be necessary.

If they only vary by 1 or 2 mm, do not bother to change them, they will ease together when you are sewing them.

CHAPTER 11

PATTERNS

Patterns for piece crowns haven't been included but they are very easy to make. See Chapters 6 and 7 on how to draft a piece crown pattern.

Half-patterns for the basic crown, brim, beret, and peak are included in five sizes. The larger pattern pieces are spread over two pages so it will be necessary to join the patterns on the respective broken line.

See Chapter 8, page 57 for transferring patterns.

Headband/bandeau for the basic beret and beret (2), see chapter 3 page 26.

THE BASIC BRIM (FRONT SECTION)

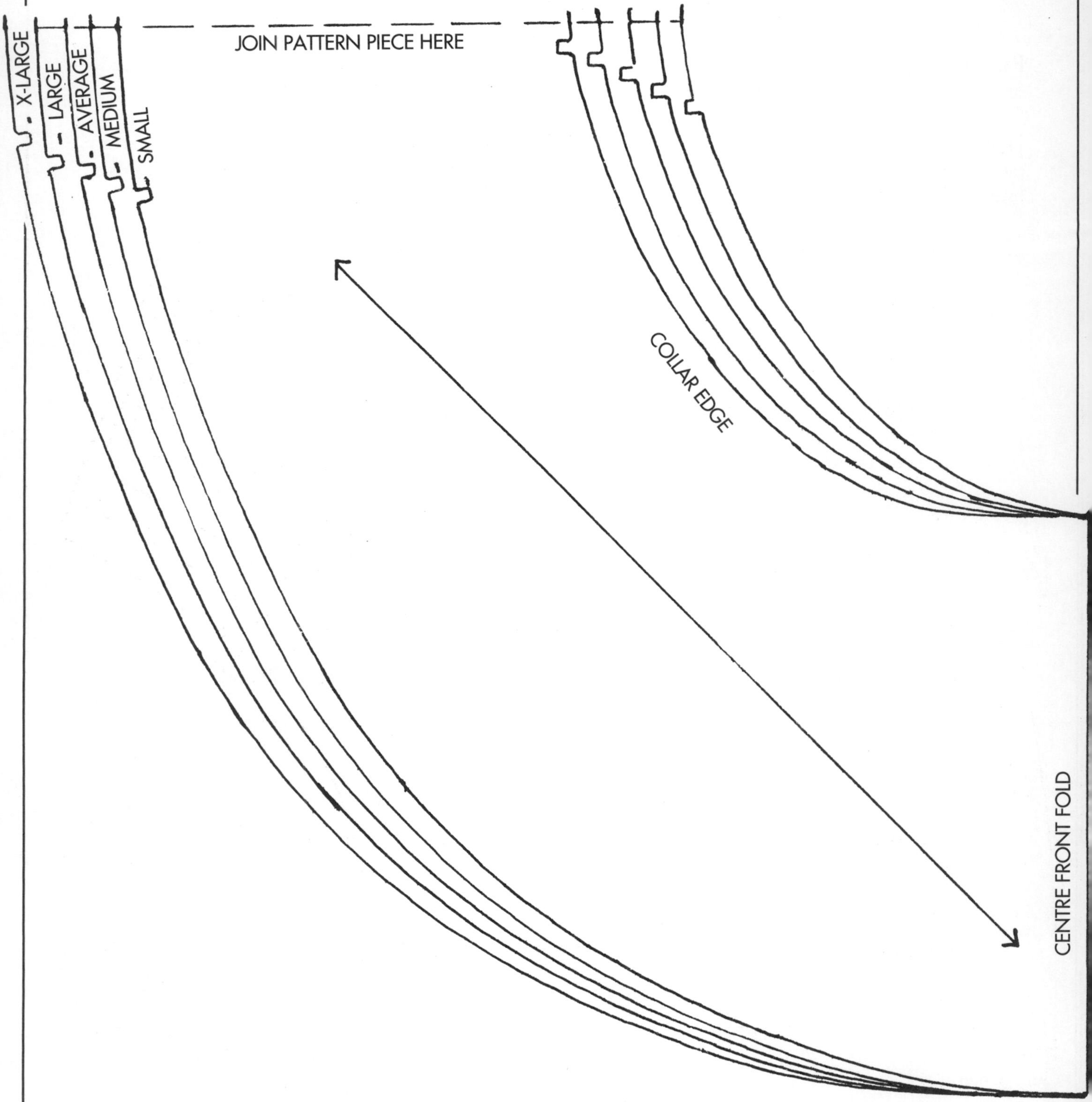

JOIN PATTERN PIECE HERE

X-LARGE

LARGE

AVERAGE

MEDIUM

SMALL

COLLAR EDGE

CENTRE FRONT FOLD

THE BASIC BRIM (BACK SECTION)

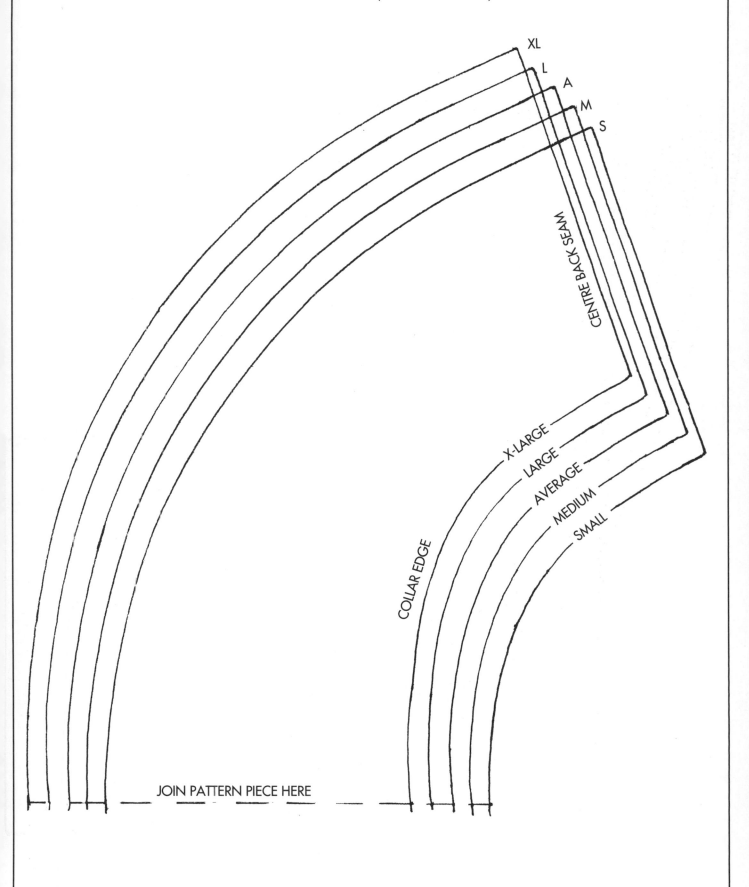

XL

L

A

M

S

CENTRE BACK SEAM

COLLAR EDGE

X-LARGE

LARGE

AVERAGE

MEDIUM

SMALL

JOIN PATTERN PIECE HERE

THE BASIC SIDE CROWN (FRONT SECTION)

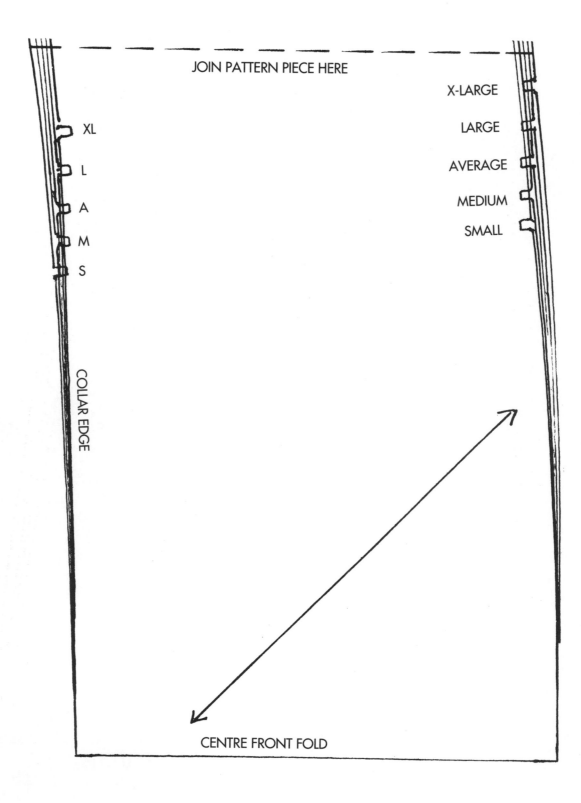

JOIN PATTERN PIECE HERE

X-LARGE

XL

LARGE

L

AVERAGE

A

MEDIUM

M

SMALL

S

COLLAR EDGE

CENTRE FRONT FOLD

THE BASIC SIDE CROWN (BACK SECTION)

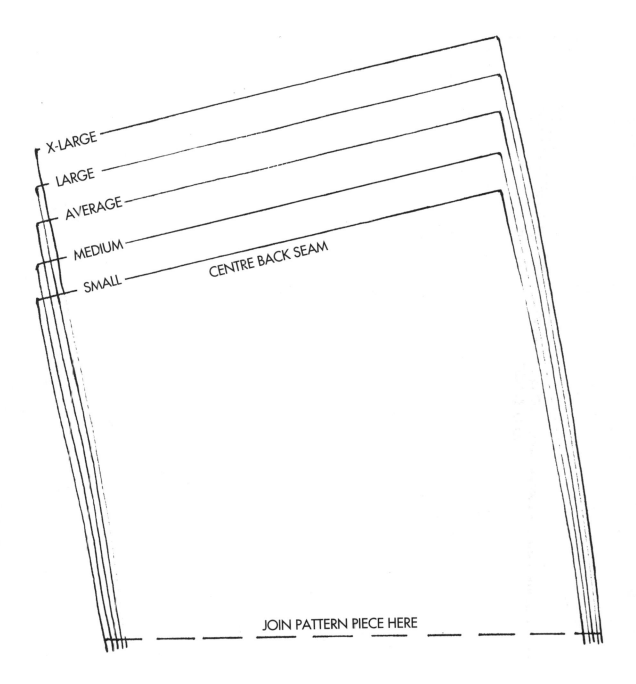

X-LARGE

LARGE

AVERAGE

MEDIUM

SMALL

CENTRE BACK SEAM

JOIN PATTERN PIECE HERE

THE BASIC COLLAR OR TOP CROWN

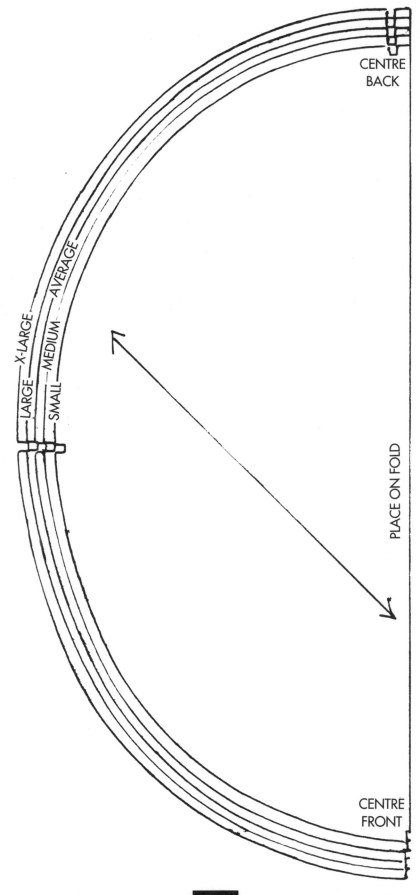

CENTRE
BACK

LARGE — X-LARGE — AVERAGE
SMALL — MEDIUM

PLACE ON FOLD

CENTRE
FRONT

THE BASIC BERET – UNDER BERET (BACK SECTION)

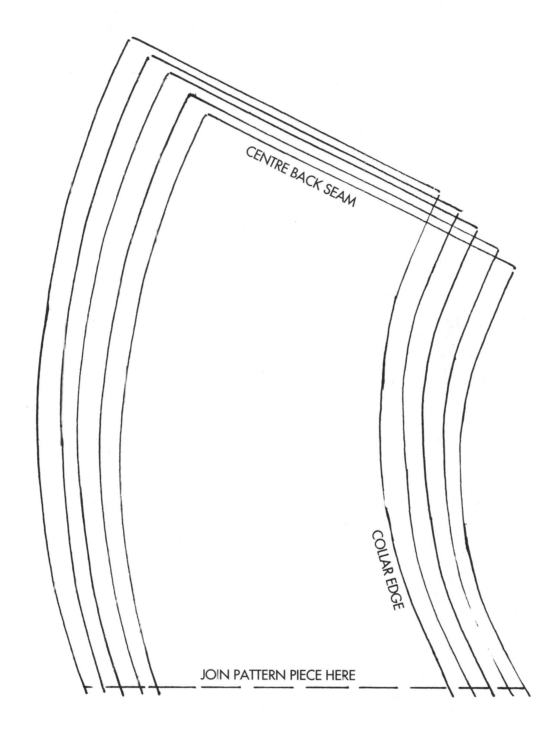

CENTRE BACK SEAM

COLLAR EDGE

JOIN PATTERN PIECE HERE

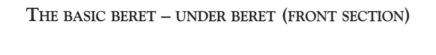

THE BASIC BERET – UNDER BERET (FRONT SECTION)

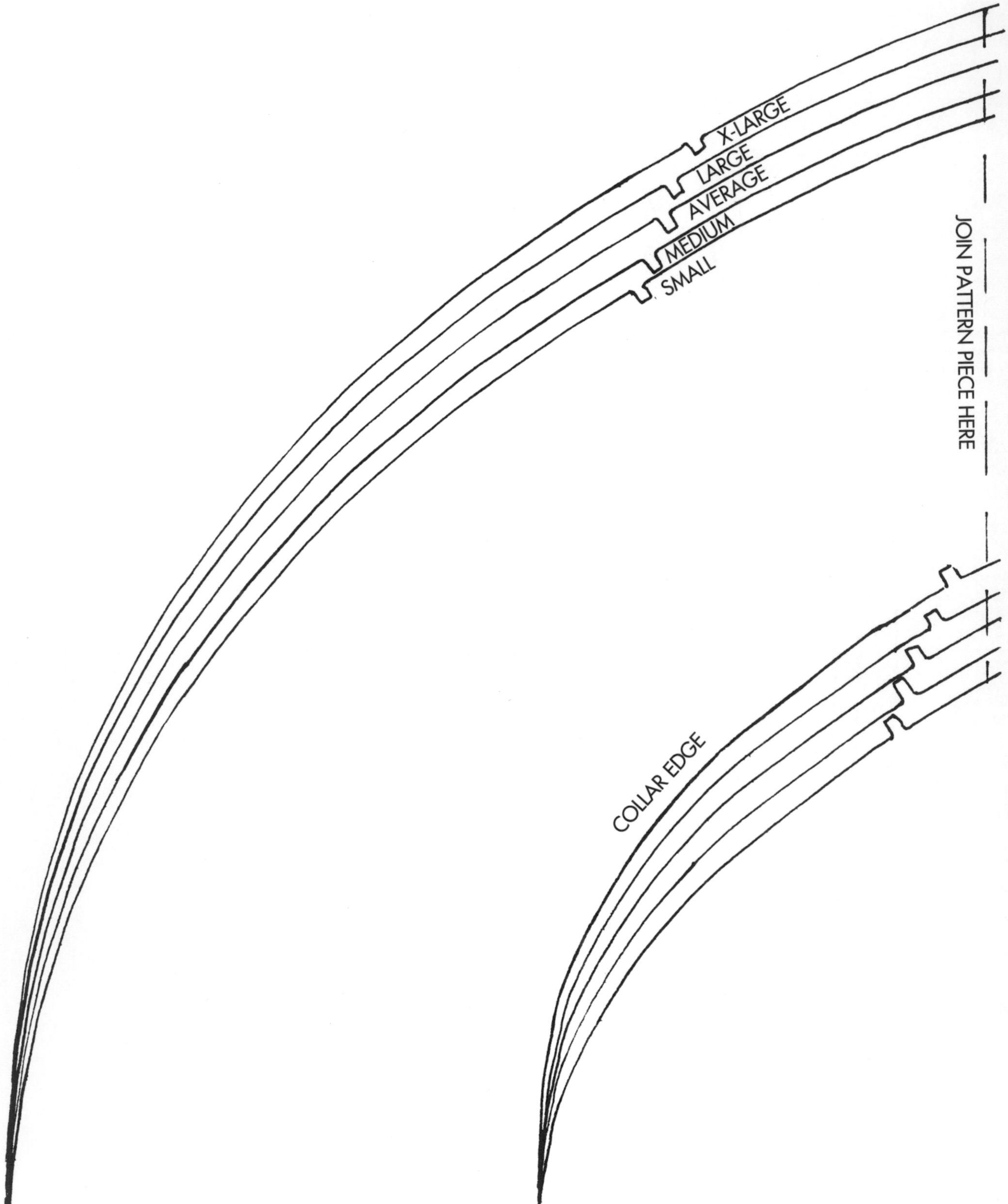

X-LARGE

LARGE

AVERAGE

MEDIUM

SMALL

JOIN PATTERN PIECE HERE

COLLAR EDGE

CENTRE FRONT FOLD

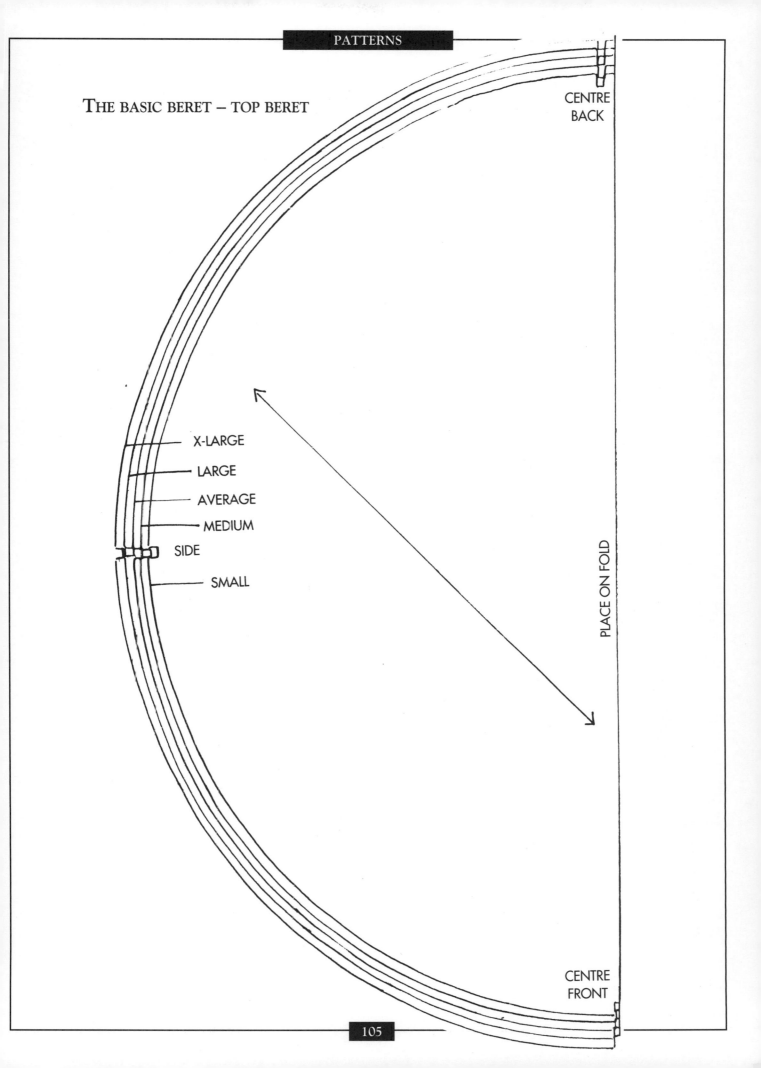

THE BASIC BERET – TOP BERET

CENTRE
BACK

X-LARGE

LARGE

AVERAGE

MEDIUM

SIDE

SMALL

PLACE ON FOLD

CENTRE
FRONT

THE BASIC PEAK

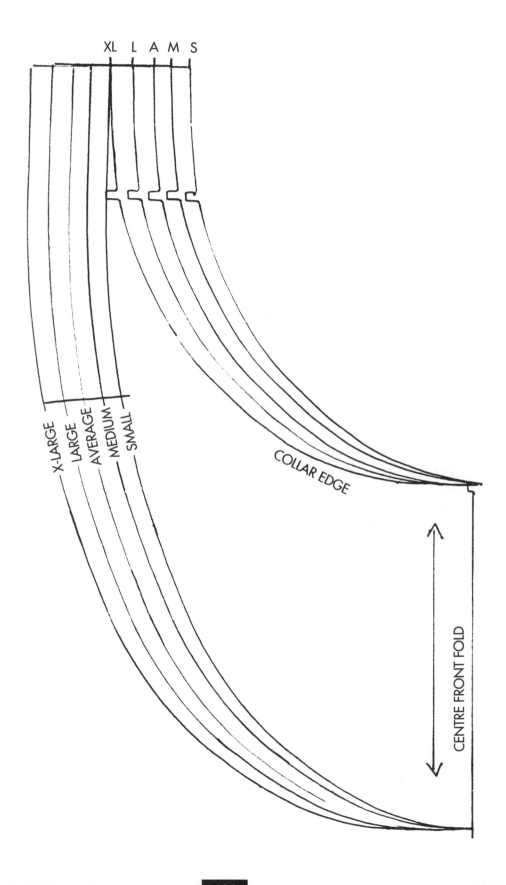

XL L A M S

X-LARGE
LARGE
AVERAGE
MEDIUM
SMALL

COLLAR EDGE

CENTRE FRONT FOLD

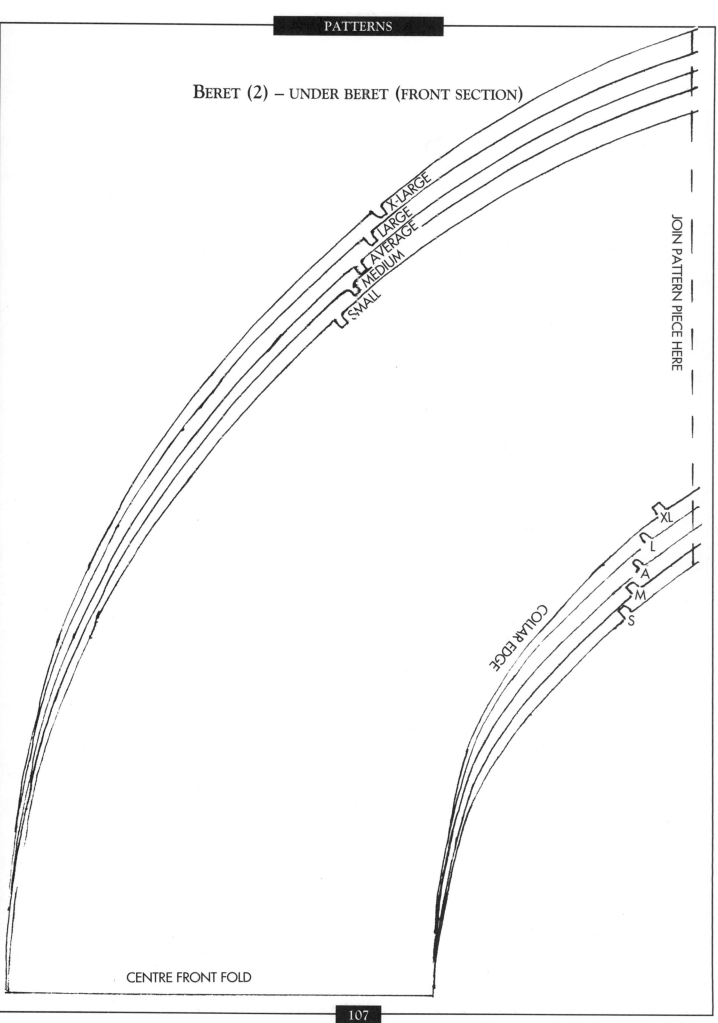

BERET (2) – UNDER BERET (FRONT SECTION)

X-LARGE
LARGE
AVERAGE
MEDIUM
SMALL

XL
L
A
M
S

JOIN PATTERN PIECE HERE

COLLAR EDGE

CENTRE FRONT FOLD

BERET (2) – UNDER BERET (BACK SECTION)

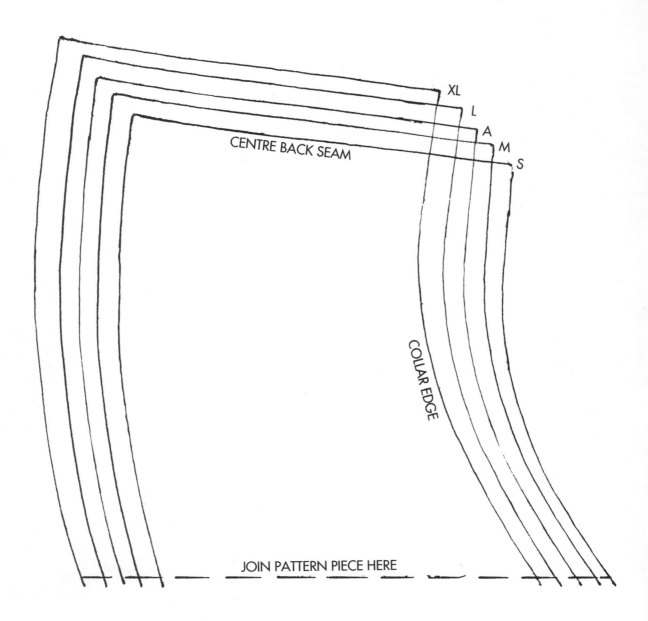

XL

L

A

M

S

CENTRE BACK SEAM

COLLAR EDGE

JOIN PATTERN PIECE HERE

BERET (2) – TOP BERET (FRONT SECTION)

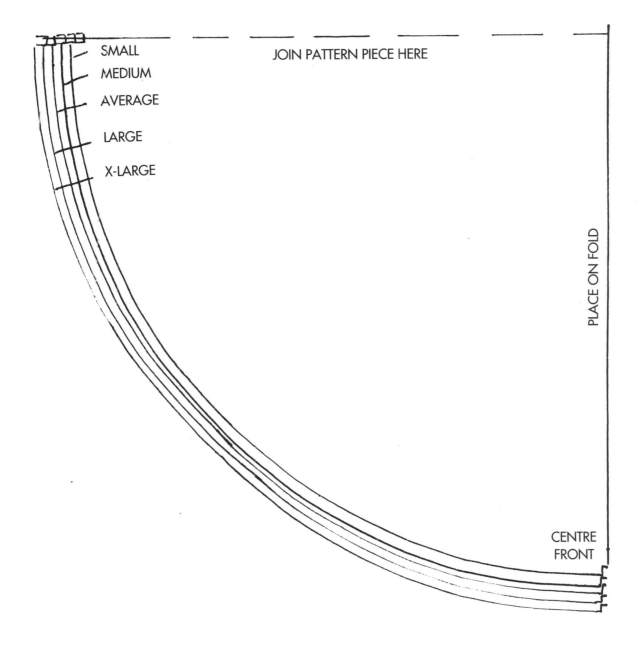

SMALL

MEDIUM

AVERAGE

LARGE

X-LARGE

JOIN PATTERN PIECE HERE

PLACE ON FOLD

CENTRE
FRONT

Beret (2) – top beret (back section)

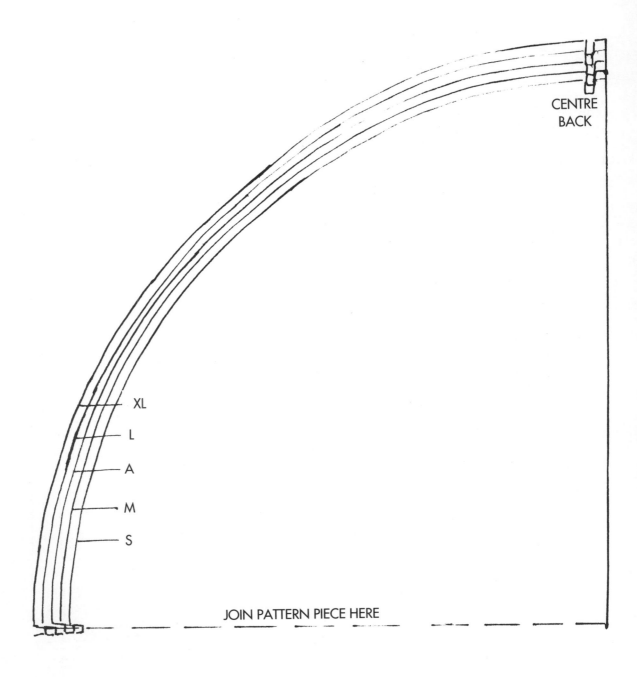

XL

L

A

M

S

CENTRE
BACK

JOIN PATTERN PIECE HERE

PEAK (2)

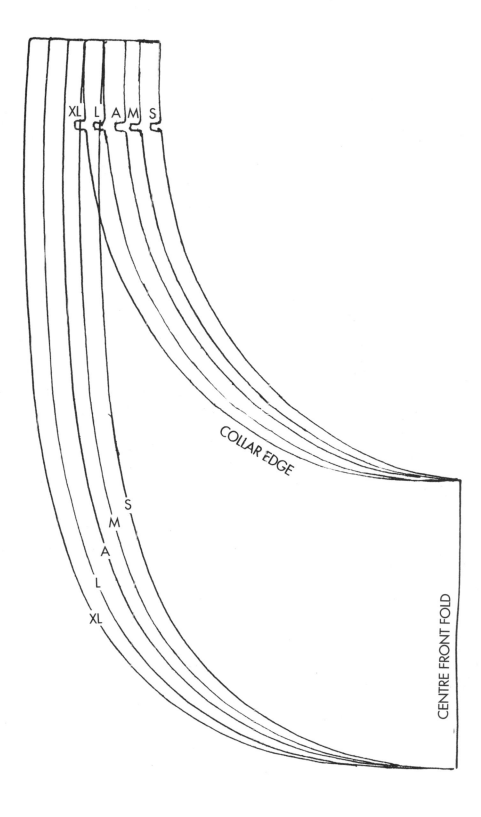

XL L A M S

COLLAR EDGE

S
M
A
L
XL

CENTRE FRONT FOLD

CHAPTER 12

MODIFYING PATTERNS

The basic brim and basic crown can be modified to some extent. First, cut a paper duplicate of the pattern piece you are to modify.

THE BASIC BRIM

ALTERING THE WIDTH

You can make an adjustment at the brim edge but it is recommended that no more than 5 cm (2") be added to or taken from the brim edge of the basic brim design. If you alter the brim size either way by more than 5 cm (2"), you can create distortions in the shape.

For a shorter or narrower brim, measure the required amount in from the brim edge.

For a wider or bigger brim, measure the required amount out from the brim edge.

The basic pattern shapes are symmetrical, so it is only necessary to modify one side of the pattern piece.

Do not alter the collar edge measurement because it must remain equal to the crown. (diagram 1)

ALTERING THE SHAPE

The basic brim can be altered so that it sits closer to the face or sits out more.

1

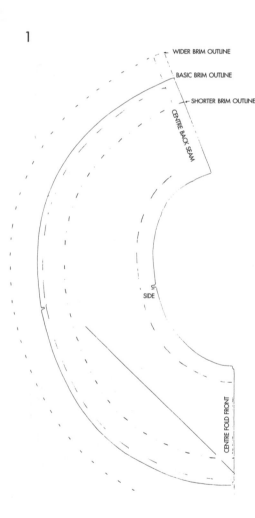

WIDER BRIM OUTLINE

BASIC BRIM OUTLINE

SHORTER BRIM OUTLINE

CENTRE BACK SEAM

SIDE

CENTRE FOLD FRONT

CLOSER TO THE FACE

Cut a paper duplicate of the pattern piece you are to modify.

Draw a line joining the side notch at the collar edge and the brim edge. Measure and mark halfway between this line and the C/F and the C/B. Draw a line connecting these measurements. These become 'cut lines'. (diagram 2) Lay this pattern over a new piece of pattern paper.

Cut along these lines from the brim edge to within 1 mm ($^{1}/_{16}$") of the collar edge, then cut into the collar edge seam allowance to within 1 mm of the collar edge.

> ## Cut one line at a time.

Overlap the cut lines by about 0.5 cm ($^{1}/_{4}$") and fix with glue or sticky tape to paper underneath. You will notice the cut at the collar edge has opened slightly, so make sure that the collar edge line has not altered. Overlap the same amount on each of the cut lines, including the C/F. At the C/B line, overlap only half the amount, 0.25 cm ($^{1}/_{8}$"). Because of the seam, this adjustment will apply to both sides at C/B. The seam allowances are already on your previous pattern piece. (diagram 3)

Diagram 4 shows how the shape of the basic brim has altered with these adjustments.

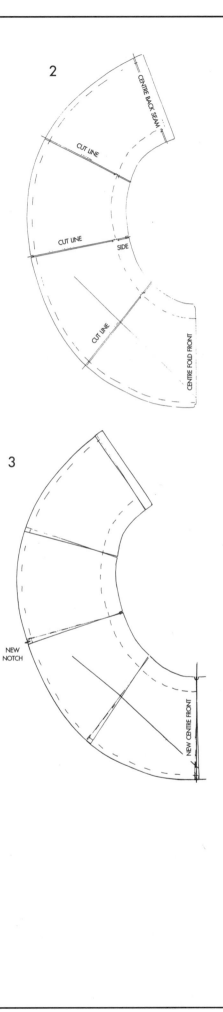

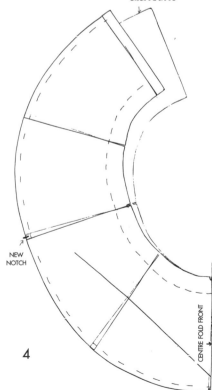

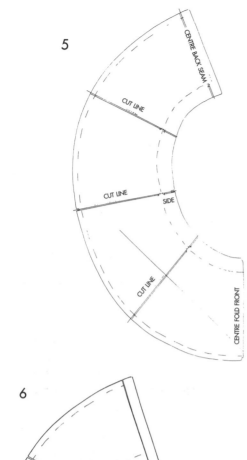

5

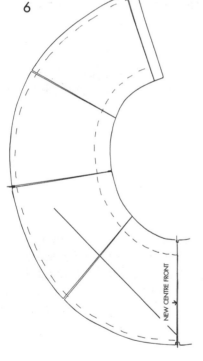

6

A FLATTER BRIM

Cut a paper duplicate of the pattern piece you are to modify.

Draw a line joining the side notch at the collar edge and the brim edge. Measure and mark halfway between this line and the C/F and the C/B. Draw a line connecting these measurements. These become 'cut lines'. (diagram 5)

Lay this pattern over a new piece of pattern paper.

Cut along these lines from the brim edge to within 1 mm (¹⁄₁₆") of the collar edge, then cut into the collar edge seam allowance to within 1 mm (¹⁄₁₆") of the collar edge. Cut one line at a time.

Open out the lines by about 0.25 cm (⅛"), and fix with glue or sticky tape to paper underneath. You will notice the cut at the collar edge has closed slightly, so make sure that the collar edge line has not altered.

Open out the same amount on each of the cut lines, including the C/F. At the C/B line open out only half the amount 1 mm (¹⁄₁₆"). Because of the seam, this adjustment will apply to both sides at C/B. The seam allowances were already on your previous pattern piece. (diagram 6)

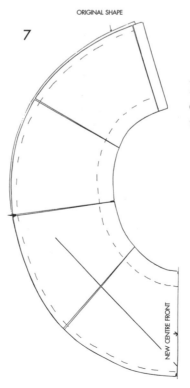

7

Diagram 7 shows how the shape of the basic brim has altered with these adjustments.

THE BASIC CROWN

Cut a paper duplicate of the pattern piece you are to modify.

The shape of the top or side crown can be increased or decreased.

The basic pattern shapes are symmetrical, so it is only necessary to modify one side of the pattern piece.

On one side of the side crown pattern, draw a line connecting the side notches at the top edge and the collar edge. Measure an equal distance between this line and C/F and C/B at the top edge and the collar edge.

8

Draw a line down connecting these marks from the top edge to the collar edge. These become the 'cut lines'. (diagram 8)

On these cut lines, cut from the top edge of side crown to within 1 mm ($\frac{1}{16}$") of the collar edge, then from the bottom edge to within 1 mm ($\frac{1}{16}$") of the collar edge.

Cut one line at a time.

INCREASING WIDTH AT TOP EDGE

Cut a paper duplicate of the pattern piece you are to modify.

Lay the pattern over a new piece of pattern paper and open the cut line to the required amount, including C/F. Little and often is the best method. Fix in place with glue or sticky tape. The collar edge seam allowance will overlap, so make sure to fix it in place. At C/B open out half the amount of the other cut lines. Because of the seam, this adjustment will apply to both sides at C/B. (diagram 9)

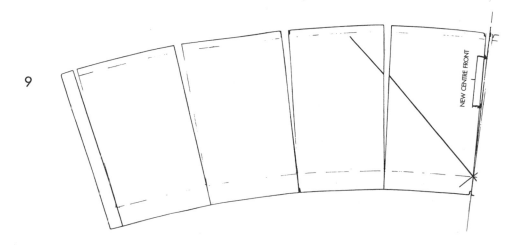

9

10

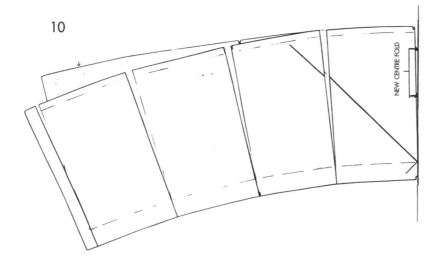

The seam allowances are already on your previous pattern piece. Diagram 10 shows how the basic side crown has altered with these adjustments.

EXTENDING BASIC CROWN HEIGHT

Cut a paper duplicate of the pattern piece you are to modify.

Fold a piece of pattern paper of suitable size in half. Place the C/F of side crown on the folded edge. Draw around the outline of the basic side crown.

In our example, we measure up from the C/F top edge 5 cm (2").

Move the side crown C/F top edge up to this point.

Draw around top edge of pattern outline, including notch, to C/B edge.

Move the C/B edge over to be in line with the C/B line of the first outline. Continue the top edge outline from this C/B to the top edge notch.

Measure halfway between the two notches – this becomes the new notch.

The seam allowances are already on your previous pattern piece. (diagram 11)

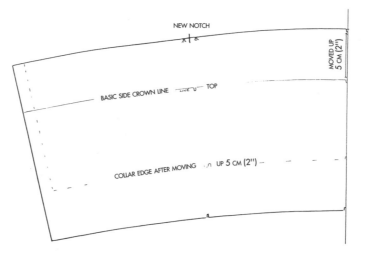

11

To shorten the basic crown height you work in the opposite direction.

INCREASING WIDTH AT TOP EDGE TO EXTENDED SIDE CROWN

Cut a paper duplicate of the pattern piece you are to modify.

In our example, we have used the extended height to crown pattern. Use the same method as in the basic side crown.

On one side of the side crown pattern, draw a line connecting the side notches at the top edge and the collar edge. Measure an equal distance between this line and C/F and C/B at the top edge and the collar edge. Draw a line connecting these marks from the top edge to the collar edge. These become the 'cut lines'. (diagram 12)

On these cut lines, cut from the top edge of side crown to within 1 mm ($^1/_{16}$") of the collar edge, then from the bottom edge to within 1 mm ($^1/_{16}$") of the collar edge.

Cut one line at a time.

Lay the pattern over a new piece of pattern paper and open the cut line to the required amount, including C/F. Little and often is the best method. Fix in place with sticky tape. The collar edge seam allowance will overlap, so make sure to fix in place. At C/B open out half the amount of the other cut lines. Because of the seam, this adjustment will apply to both sides at C/B. (diagram 13)

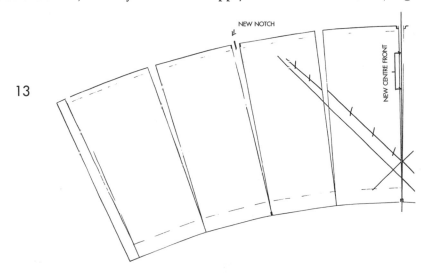

The seam allowances are already on your previous pattern piece.

Diagram 14 shows how the shape of the extended side crown has altered with these adjustments.

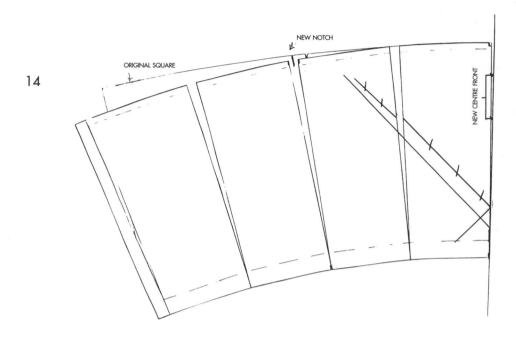

14

DECREASING WIDTH AT TOP EDGE

Cut a paper duplicate of the pattern piece you are to modify.

In our example, we have used the extended height to side crown pattern. On one side of the side crown pattern, draw a line connecting the side notches at the top edge and the collar edge. Measure an equal distance between this line and C/F and C/B at the top edge and the collar edge. Draw a line connecting these marks from the top edge to the collar edge. These become the 'cut lines'. (diagram 15)

15

Lay the pattern over a new piece of pattern paper and overlap the cut line to the required amount, including C/F. Little and often is the best method. Fix in place with sticky tape. The collar edge seam allowance will open out, so be sure to fix in place. At C/B open cut half the amount of the other cut lines. Because of the seam, this adjustment will apply to both sides at C/B.

The seam allowances are already on your previous pattern piece.

Diagram 16 shows how the shape of the extended side crown has altered with these adjustments.

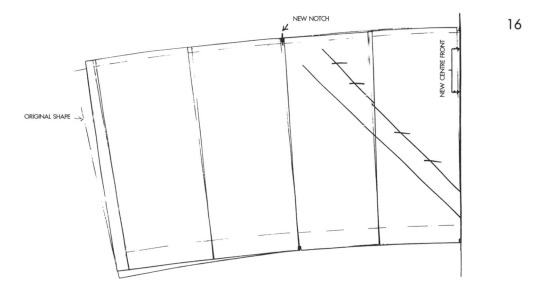

TRANSFERRING PATTERN SHAPES

Lay the modified pattern over a new piece of folded pattern paper, C/F on folded edge. Pin in place, then cut out new pattern shape.

The seam allowances are already on your previous pattern piece.

To avoid a dip up or down, 'square' edge in from C/F by 0.75 cm (¼" to ⅜") at both the collar and opposite edge of each pattern piece. (diagram 17)

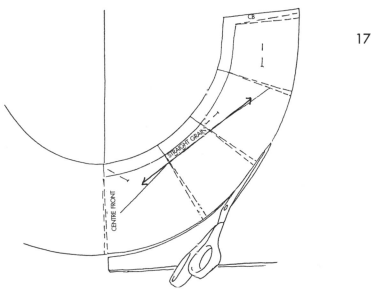